Serial Killers &
The Aftermath

Serial Killers &
The Aftermath

~

Rosemary J. Erickson Ph.D.
Forensic Sociologist

Copyright © 2018 Rosemary J. Erickson PhD
Published by Athena Research Corporation
CreateSpace Independent Publishing Platform

ISBN: 1983402869
ISBN-13: 978-1983402869

To my husband, Arnie Stenseth, who
helped make and tell some of the stories.

Perhaps I know best why man is the only animal that laughs. He alone suffers so excruciatingly that he was compelled to invent laughter.

Friedrich Nietzsche (1844-1900)

CONTENTS

TABLE OF FIGURES

ACKNOWLEGEMENTS

Building a safer society takes the efforts of everyone—families, schools, communities, and agencies. I want to thank my fellow forensic researchers, psychologist, and sociologists, as well as security managers, expert witnesses, lawyers, judges, and law enforcement for their efforts in working to make this world more secure. I also acknowledge the positive efforts made by corporations, government, and associations, and I hope that will continue.

A special thanks is in order for Clark Matthews, who was president and CEO of 7-Eleven, and that company was the leader in crime prevention.

In addition, I want to thank my professors at the American University in Washington, D. C. for having such a positive influence on my research and career in expert witnessing. I owe gratitude to so many of my friends, who are interested in my cases and writing, and have helped me with their feedback.

Of course, thanks goes to my family--my father, mother, two brothers, two nieces, three nephews, and their spouses. Criminological research has always been a family affair with me and has extended into the next generation with my family and my step-children and step-grandchildren.

PREFACE

Four of the serial killer cases, for which I was an expert witness in the civil suits, are the centerpiece of this book. As a forensic sociologist and expert witness, I am involved in the aftermath of such a violent event. I may be hired either as a defense expert witness or a plaintiff's expert witness, when a civil suit follows a violent event, such as these serial killings. Depending upon the location in which the murder or rape happens, the location's owner may be sued in a premises liability suit claiming lack of security and not providing a safe environment. My research on the case includes understanding the mind of the perpetrator and how and why he selected a particular place or victim. How did I get into this?

As a young woman, I was inspired to be a researcher by an anthropological novel called *Return to Laughter*. It was written in the 1950s, by a female anthropologist. I was so impressed with the fact that she was doing field work in Nigeria, alone, living in a hut, among the "natives", but it turned out that it was in fact a *fictional* account of her anthropological study in Nigeria, and she was living with her husband. I later learned that when I worked with her husband, also an anthropologist, that she was not there alone. He was with her the entire time, working on the same project and living in the same hut.

He added "She just wrote me out of the book". By then, they were divorced, so, "She actually wrote me out of her life." According to sociologist David Riesman, in the foreword to the 1964 edition, what she did was to follow in the footsteps of Descartes by taking the reader into her confidence to explain how she arrived at her discoveries.[1] By bringing the human element into this book, which is a sociological novel, my hope is that it could inspire young men and women to become forensic sociologists or at the very least to think like sociologists, in an effort to better understand our society and to learn how with information comes change.

Sociology is the study of people in interaction with other people and institutions. Forensic sociology applies those concepts to the law. I am writing this book in a personal, first-person, sometimes fictionalized account, so this is my opportunity to tell you, the reader, what it is like, in my own words. It has been a wonderful life of studying people. In fact, at a poetry reading a few years ago, among the readers of Shakespeare, Bronte, and Keates, I chose to read a poem from the American Sociological Association about "How Glad I am to be a Sociologist".

The legal cases, of which I write, are inspired by true events but some are fictionalized, and the names of the victims, criminals, lawyers, judges, locations, and cities are sometimes changed to protect both the innocent and the guilty. For the reader, I say, please just take a ride with me and understand that this story is my reality, which is an important lesson that I learned from my husband's psychiatrist.

I went to a session with my husband, Arnie, in 2003, when he was agonizing over the war in Iraq. He told the psychiatrist that when the jets and helicopters would fly overhead at our beautiful beach home in San Diego on their training missions, he would seize up with anger about the senseless killings in Iraq. I told the psychiatrist: "I see and hear the exact same helicopters and think with relief of how they are protecting us". The psychiatrist took a deep breath, looked at me, and then quietly said: "That is your reality, and this is his reality. We are here about his reality," This book is my reality.

An earlier book of mine--*Prairie Patriarch: A Farmer's Daughter Who Becomes an Expert Witness on Violent Crime*--is about my father and the changes in the Norwegian-American farm family in South Dakota in the early to the mid-1900's. It is also about my "roots" and how I became who I am, which is a forensic sociologist, researcher, and expert witness on violent crime. The answer is that at the root of it all was the prairie patriarch--my father—who died in 1980 at age 77. The nurturing by my mother continued for twenty more years, until her death in the year 2000 at age 88.

The story of my "roots" essentially ends with that book, while I was still with my husband and mentor, Dr. Bud Crow, a social psychologist, who died in 1989. After his death, I married a college acquaintance, Arnie Stenseth, an actor. Both of these men shaped my professional career with their constant support, encouragement, and love. This book reflects briefly on my

iv

childhood and then picks up with the 1960s with my career in research and how that led to my becoming an expert witness in violent crime.

For the next two decades, beginning in the 1990s, I was an expert witness in some of the most heinous crime cases in the country, and I will share with the reader how a female survives in a man's world of criminal violence, security, law enforcement, and the justice system. I considered calling this book "Call Dr. Erickson". The concept of "Call Dr. Erickson" is three-fold. One is that this is what one lawyer says to another when referring me on a case. They will say: "Call Dr. Erickson because she is the expert in premises liability security cases and why the perpetrators do what they do". The second reason comes from the admonition at trial from the Judge: "Call Dr. Erickson to the stand", followed by the court reporter saying: "Raise your right hand. Do you swear to tell the truth the whole truth and nothing but the truth, so help you, God?" The third reason is that my dissertation advisor for my Ph.D. said you will get dinner reservations at a restaurant more quickly if you tell them to: "Call Dr. Erickson".

INTRODUCTION

Being a sociologist is a way of thinking about the world and is the sum total of your life experiences along with what you are taught and what you learn. It is cumulative. It is chronological, and it occurs in historical context. Marx, for example, is criticized for not fighting for equal rights for women, but consider the historical context in which he lived and wrote. In the 19th century, there were not equal rights for women. They did not have the vote. Another frequently asked question is; "What is the difference between psychology and sociology?" The short and simple answer is that psychology is the study of individuals, and sociology is the study of individuals in interaction with other individuals in society and in the institutions of school, church, family, organizations, associations and work.

A parent may have two children, completely different from each other, and say: "But I did the same thing with both of them," but you didn't. First, they had a different birth order and were born in different seasons, months, years, historical contexts, and environments. Most importantly, each one reacted differently to you, and before the child came out of the womb, that child already had a unique genetic difference and a distinct disposition. After a lifetime of studying people, I am convinced that disposition is, in fact, the single most important indicator of how a person will live their lives in interaction with others and with themselves. You know who you are: Those who wake up grouchy, versus the ones who wake up happy, and those in-between. Many parents will tell you, "They came out of the womb that way".

I actually started out with the study of psychology, getting my B.A. in Psychology. I then switched to sociology when I learned that I didn't want to work directly with individuals, but rather indirectly through research and their interaction with each other. I received my Master's in Sociology and my Ph.D. in Sociology and Justice. My research led to criminological research specifically, and ultimately to expert witnessing in premises liability civil suits, resulting from violent crime. My cases are civil cases and are always the result of a criminal act, usually violent,

1

like the rape of a guest in a hotel.

The hotel is then sued, and I testify either for the plaintiff (the victim) or for the defense (the hotel) about whether or not they had done all they should have done as far as security to prevent the incident and whether the victim played a role in their own demise. My field is forensic sociology. Forensic sociology is the application of sociology to the law. Forensic means --"the law"--so I have defined my career as forensic sociology, rather than criminology. It also is not criminal profiling, like the FBI does.

Sociological profiling studies the perpetrator, the victim, and the place; whereas FBI criminal profiling studies the perpetrator and victim, but primarily the perpetrator. I study the perpetrator but also the victim and place. I look at why he did it, and what may or may not have prevented him from doing it. I say "he" because 90% of violence in our society, and throughout history in all societies, is perpetrated by males. At the same time, I need to understand the victim and what part they may have played in causing the event. For example, a homicide in a bar fight may be the result of the perpetrator and the victim becoming intoxicated. One of them ends up dead. I seek to understand whether the interaction of the alcohol and the resulting mutual combatancy led to the individual's death.

What stands out most about the sum total of over 200 cases I have done is the resiliency of the human spirit, and how the victims and their families have managed to survive and pull their lives back together. But there are also the perpetrators and their families. Until we decide to and learn how to rehabilitate the criminals, we have very little hope for changing them or society.

Understanding the criminal's background helps me to understand who they are, why they did it, and what would have kept them from committing the crime. The childhood circumstances that led them to where they are and to what they do are nearly beyond comprehension. I'm struck that people often say, "It's up to the parents," to which I reply, "Have you seen the parents?" How naïve that we should think the parents are going to make the difference when they themselves may be drugged-out, doped up, or mentally unstable. When we save our children, we save our own future. It's all about the children.

When I see one of my cases, I see both the victim and the victim's family and the perpetrator and the perpetrator's family. I am struck by the fact that often the most frequent comment that the perpetrator's mother makes is: "But he was a good boy." No, he wasn't. At the same time, the family may be fine, but the boy ends up as a "bad boy". I see the suffering of the perpetrator's family, along with that of the victim and the victim's family. Rarely do I see the perpetrator's self-recrimination. Sometimes it is denial, but sometimes it's just lack of empathy, and I am convinced that sociopathy, sometimes called psychopathy, is at the root of much of the violence that we see perpetrated in our society today. Some of violence is uniquely American and grows out of our Wild West past, and violence is also deeply rooted in slavery.

Most of what I have learned about crime, I learned from criminals themselves, such as the notorious robber Ray Johnson, who was on my staff. At one point, on my staff, I had robbers, rapists, and murderers. If you want to know about something, you go to the source. For me, as a sociologist, the source is the criminal. For that reason, each decade of my professional career, I have followed up with surveys and interviews with criminals, now numbering over one thousand participants. In each criminal case where the perpetrator has been caught, I try to interview him or them, if possible, or at least pore through the criminal history, psychiatric evaluation, and childhood history.

My understanding of crime and criminals comes from them, but my interest in why people do what they do began in my childhood spent on a farm, with hours of solitude to contemplate the workings of the world around me. I was not particularly interested in why or how the stars aligned when I looked upward. I wasn't particularly interested in how the crops grew, or how the birds flew overhead, or how the fish swam in the river winding its way through our farm. I was a sociologist even then, because what I cared about was why a schoolchild in my one-room school was mean to another student; or why one learned so quickly and the other not; why some were rich and others were poor; how some parents were strict, and others were not. My two older brothers were so different from each other and different from me, and our parents were different from each

3

other, and we were different from them. I also had a lot of interest in ant colonies. Living on a sand hill, on a farm called Turner Hill, I could watch their activity for hours, comparing it to the humans with whom I lived. These are the things you do growing up on a farm. There is a lot of alone time.

I started my schooling in first grade in a one-room school on the corner of our farm. We did not have kindergarten. My husband Arnie now says to me: "Think what you could have done, if you had gone to kindergarten." I went from a farm to receiving a Ph.D. in Sociology and Justice from the American University in WDC to advising President Obama's election campaign on criminal justice. I have dined with Stalin's daughter, Svetlana, and danced around a room with her daughter--Stalin's granddaughter, Olga, when she was but six years old. I would later experience Svetlana's wrath in her letters to me, when she thought I was trying to steal her daughter from her. I've met with Interpol and studied terrorists and terrorism, working executive protection during the Los Angeles Olympics in 1984 and in Mexico after that. I have gone into maximum security prisons and talked to truly evil, frightening individuals. I have visited crime sites that are as threatening in the daytime as they are at night; and testified in courtrooms where every judge is a different character and personality, as are the lawyers, on both sides.

I have worked with and met famous academicians and politicians, as well as media celebrities. And to this day, I continue to *become a sociologist* because I am convinced that every day changes you in some way as an individual, and in many ways as a sociologist. I would like to do it all over again. Only this time, I would like to start out with a cell phone, a computer and the internet, instead of outdoor plumbing, no telephone, and no electricity. I loved the way I grew up, but I can't imagine who I would be today if I had done it with a computer *and* kindergarten. That is perhaps the best example of what I mean by historical context.

Each decade in which we live can be characterized by a few distinctive events or characteristics – such as music, inventions, presidents, literature, movies, and fashion. Some, if not all, decades have a defining major social event, war, or personal

4

event. In sum, there are no free passes and it does not all come out even; and life is neither fair, nor just. We have no choice about our beginnings, but there are some things we can do with them. This book is about what I did.

INTRODUCTION

CHAPTER ONE

~

BEGINNINGS

Raised in a rural area, with no electricity, no indoor plumbing, no telephone, and reading by the light of a kerosene lamp—no, that is not just a description of Abraham Lincoln, in 1809; it is my life from birth to six years of age, from 1942 to 1948, on a farm south of Davis, South Dakota. In rural South Dakota, we did not get electricity or indoor plumbing until 1948. The Rural Electrification Association (REA) ushered in a whole new era, a brave new world, in which our family farm, and others around us for the first time had indoor plumbing, running water, power, lights, electricity, and a refrigerator instead of an ice box. The Saturday night ritual of taking a bath in a tin tub in front of a coal-burning stove was over. Going outside to an outdoor toilet in the middle of the night in a blizzard was over. Using the Sears Roebuck or Montgomery Ward catalogs as toilet paper in that outside toilet was over.

The telephone line had been brought into our farm a year before then, in 1947, when I was five years old. That was probably the single most important early factor in my eventually becoming a sociologist. As a farm kid, you rarely saw other kids besides your siblings, and the telephone was the new great communicator, especially because of the "party line". The party line included several farm families on one line, and you could listen in to other conversations. Everyone knew there was no privacy in a telephone conversation in Turner County in the 40's. When someone else's phone rang, you heard it. Each farm had a number with a distinctive, loud, and audible ring. The Dewey Erickson family's ring was one long ring, followed by two short rings, referred to as, "one long and two shorts".

Before Dad (Dewey) went to the field in the morning the phone installers were due to come, he said: "Opal, make sure they hang it up high enough so the kids can't reach it." So, she had it placed high on the southeast wall of the dining room, not realizing that since I was a climber, I could go from the chair to the dining room buffet with alacrity and easily reach the phone.

If our phone rang, I always answered it if I was within two rooms of it because I could get there first. If I heard anyone else's ring, I also quickly crawled up on the buffet, carefully and quietly pulling the black receiver off the hook of the phone, and listening to everything being said.

The party line provided a jackpot of information. At five years of age, I knew more about my community than my parents did and could fill them and my two older brothers in on all the details over the supper table at night. I could tell them who was talking to whom, where people were going, and when they were going there. Sometimes, though, I would get busted by the people on the line, like when my Godmother Alma would say: "Rosemary, are you on the line?" Because I was from the Midwest, and because we were Lutherans, and because it was a rural area, we were taught to be honest, so after a short pause, I would reluctantly say:

"Yes, Alma."

"You need to hang up now."

"Okay, Alma", and I would hang up. Who needs wire-tapping if you have a party line?

Everyone knew others were listening in on their conversations, and they knew who listened the most. I don't think any men ever listened in, but we knew which women listened in, and as far as I know, I was the only other kid that had that kind of interest in gathering data. An anthropologist will gather bones, a geologist will gather stones, but a sociologist will gather information. From those early conversations, I not only learned factual information, but I learned about relationships, reactions, and the rural farm philosophy of the 40s.

You must listen hard to Midwesterners, for example, and ask a lot of questions, to get anything out of them directly because they don't say a lot in the first place. They are generally not reflective or introspective when they do say something. I was very interested in what people were doing but even more interested in what they were thinking. I loved eavesdropping on Saturday nights too, but not on the telephone. That was when my parents would have friends over to play cards, and they would talk late into the night. More soothing than the pharmaceuticals of today, I would go to sleep listening to the steady murmur of their voices, punctuated with laughter and lively discussions of their childhoods and lives, while feeling very safe in my cocoon. To this day, I prefer, the low mumbling of people having a good time, rather than quiet at night.

Born in South Dakota in 1942, I lived on a farm near Davis, South Dakota with my parents and two older brothers for my first fourteen years. It is about 35 miles southeast of Sioux Falls, South Dakota, and it is the opposite side of the state from Mt. Rushmore (over 300 miles away). If someone has been to South Dakota, it is usually to the "other side of the state". Both my father and mother were born in southeastern South Dakota, the farming side—not the ranching side of the state. My mother was born Opal Magnuson, and grew up in Elk Point, South Dakota. My father was Dewey Erickson and grew up on a farm by Centerville, South Dakota.

Both Dewey and Opal's grandparents had emigrated from Norway in the late 1800s to farm in South Dakota. Mother's ancestors were from Bergen, and Father's family was from Trondheim. Our family was Norwegian Lutheran, and I thought everyone else was too for a long time. I also thought that South Dakota was in the center of the United States and only later learned, that it wasn't geographically the center, but it was politically the "center". I attended a one-room country school through fifth grade. By that time, there were only five students left in the school, so it was like a tutorial program with personal attention from the teacher and learning from the older students and their studies. The school was on the corner of our farm in Southeastern South Dakota, near Davis (population 100— most of the time). Grades six through eight were in Centerville (population 1,200—most of the time). Centerville was ten miles from our farm. I went to school in "town" from sixth grade to ninth grade. Students were distinguished between farm kids and town kids, and we thought the town kids had it so much better than we did because they had each other. They agreed.

My schooling in Centerville changed in 1957, in ninth grade, when my father decided to move our family to San Diego, California. Up to then, this was the most traumatic experience of my life. There, I attended Horace Mann junior high and Crawford High School in San Diego. I went from a class of 23 in

Centerville to one with over 700 students in California. What I feared was a disaster from which I would never recover turned out wonderfully, however. I had wonderful new friends, and then, just before my senior year, my father decided to move us back to the farm. The second most traumatic experience of my life was moving back to the farm in South Dakota from California. Again, I thought life would end, as only a 16 year-old-girl can dramatize it, but I had a wonderful senior year, and graduated from Centerville, High School the following spring in 1960. After high school graduation, you would have thought I'd go back to San Diego, but instead I attended Augustana College (now Augustana University) in Sioux Falls, South Dakota, receiving my B. A. in Psychology in 1964.

After graduation, I worked as a state mental health representative for the State of South Dakota Department of Health at the state capitol in Pierre, South Dakota. The effort there was to create community organizations and agencies to support mental health patients and allow them to live in their communities, rather than in state mental hospitals—a hard sell in rural communities in the 1960s. Also, I had to stay overnight in the mental institution and found that not to my liking. That was way too "up close and personal" for me.

After a year of that work, I moved back to San Diego. I packed my mother and everything I owned into my white 1965 2-door Mustang, and we headed for California. She flew back home after a few weeks, leaving me there with no idea what I was going to do for a living, but I quickly picked up work. I contracted with a non-profit organization and wrote a technical report entitled: *Pockets of Poverty*. For the State of California, I wrote a study of mental health catchment areas and found they were mostly in the *ghettos* (I will use that word throughout, as it was used in this historical context). Those scooped up for mental health reasons were mostly black and poor. (I will use black or African-American interchangeably, based on historical context). That combined research proved fortuitous in landing me my dream job in 1966, at a California think tank--Western Behavioral Sciences Institute (WBSI). The Institute was located near the beautiful beach and Pacific Ocean in La Jolla, CA.

CHAPTER TWO

~

WBSI

When I initially interviewed at Western Behavioral Sciences Institute (WBSI), in 1966, I wanted to make sure that I was hired for my brains and not hired for my looks. Previous bosses had made unwanted advances, which was typical of the 1960s and earlier (and now). At age 23, for my interview with Dr. Wayman J. (Bud) Crow, the Associate Director of WBSI, I wore a skirt below the knee (not a 1960s mini-skirt), a matching top that covered everything, low pumps (really boring), pulled my long blond hair back into a "stern teacher" bun, and wore glasses instead of contacts. He hired me on the spot and asked me to start work the following Monday. He said it was a 'no brainer" (or whatever the expression was then) because of my work on poverty that completely qualified me for the War on Poverty contract, on which I would work. He hired me on Friday, and I went to work on Monday.

When I went to work on Monday, a fellow staff member, an elderly gentleman, who was a physicist and benefactor of the Institute, saw me pull up to the door. He had seen me at the interview earlier and later reported his observations to me. He said I pulled up in my white Mustang right in front of the office building front door. He saw my legs come out first, with high heels, followed by a very tight, short mini skirt, no glasses, and long straight blonde hair (no bun). He said, "This isn't fair because that is not what you looked like when you were interviewed." I laughed and promised him I would deliver on the "brain part."

Dr. Bud Crow was 42, and I knew about him as a famous psychologist, Professor of Psychology at San Diego State University, and founder of the Western Behavioral Sciences Institute in 1959. At the end of my first week, during a Friday morning staff meeting, Dr. Crow (Bud) made a point of telling the staff that he would need to "pick my brain" (his phraseology) on our new project, and that we would have lunch together that day and report on our findings at the next staff meeting.

In the 1960s, at WBSI, that meant drinking at lunch, which I had never done before. A few doors away, was a beautiful courtyard café with shade provided by palm trees, and a brick tile courtyard underneath other black wrought iron tables. "Rosemary, you're not in South Dakota anymore", I said to myself. Bud said he would have his usual martini, and I tried white wine at lunch for the first time, which made me feel really "freed up" shall we say? The afternoon was short because on Fridays, there was always an early staff party, following the late lunch. Bud and I lasted at the party for only a few minutes, and he suggested we leave. He later swore that I said "Yes, let's have our own party." Did I say that? I have no idea. But that is what we did that night, and we were together as a couple, for the next 23 years, until his untimely death in 1989 at age 65. He was twenty years older than I, which is just what I needed, and he was my mentor for my career.

In 1966, WBSI was one of three entities nation-wide selected to evaluate the Federal War on Poverty, and that was the project, for which I was hired. It was through that research that my interest turned more toward sociology than psychology, and I started my graduate studies in sociology at San Diego State (now San Diego State University), receiving my M. A. degree in Sociology in 1973, while working full-time at WBSI.

The evaluation of the War on Poverty brought me together with some of the top minds in the country, at universities and government, on understanding poverty, what causes it, whether it is generational, and how it can be alleviated. Two major programs that came out of the program and the evaluation were Operation Head Start and Community Action Councils, organizing at a community level to make a difference.

We used welfare recipients as staff at the Institute and in so doing brought blacks and browns (the word at that time for Hispanics) to La Jolla to work in a previously all white enclave for both work and living. In the mid-sixties, my two best friends from work, both black women, and I would go to lunch at the La Valencia, an upscale restaurant overlooking the Pacific Ocean. Heads would turn as we were seated, during the 1960s, because inter-racial "lunching" just "wasn't done" in La Jolla at that time. Hiring the poor and minorities was a way for us to provide jobs and understand the disenfranchised.

At WBSI, The evaluation of the War on Poverty transitioned in the early 1970s to a study of criminals, ex-offenders and their needs. My Master's thesis on the subject resulted in a book, with colleagues, entitled *Paroled but Not Free*. At that point, there were still attempts to rehabilitate prisoners, educate them, provide employment, and support them upon their re-entry into society. Our efforts at the Institute were in the form of real-life experiments, and we opened a half-way house for offenders, until one of the ex-offenders shot another resident of the house. That was too up close for me. We closed the house and project but kept the former convicts on our staff.

The most famous was Ray Johnson, as mentioned previously, who had been in prisons in California for 26 years for armed robbery. He had even escaped from Folsom State Prison in California. The first day he came to work for me, he said "I ain't never worked for no woman before". "Okay . . . We'll see how this goes", I thought to myself, feeling a little anxious. Later, however, we became close friends and colleagues. In fact, I visited Folsom Prison with him. From that experience, I quickly learned that prison alumnae are not popular with the guards, particularly if the prisoner had escaped, as Ray had done, even though he was recaptured a few days after that "great escape". One day, after Ray had worked at the Institute for a few months, Bud came into a meeting where Ray and others were talking.

Bud said. "We have a new contract." Ray, in his usual manner, paused a moment, looked up, and "On who?" Bud quickly explained: "No, Ray, it's not that kind of a contract. It's not the kind where you pay someone to kill someone". There was quite a learning curve for Ray Johnson to go from armed robber to prisoner for 26 years to the real world as a rehabilitated ex-con.

Archie Connett, a murderer, who had killed his three children and unsuccessfully tried to kill his wife, was on our staff at that time also. He had served his time and joined our staff when he got out of prison. We socialized with Archie a lot until he got married again and rebuilt his life. I had an interviewer on my research staff who was a rapist. He was on parole, and out of prison, but committed multiple rapes while working for me. He seemed like such a nice guy, but he would break into women's bedrooms, who were strangers, and rape them. A burglar on our staff broke into Bud's and my house one day, while he knew we were at the office, and stole Bud's razor and poker cash. He knew Bud played poker because he was one of his "Poker Buddies", as was Ray. The burglar confessed the crime to Ray, and Ray told Bud. This is why they say to never trust a con. Yet another con man, who was one of my interviewers, would use me as a reference to try to get money advanced for gambling in Las Vegas casinos. Of course, I would say "no" every time to the midnight calls I received from the casinos seeking authorization.

Another former armed robber was also on staff. He and Ray did the field work in creating our robbery and violence prevention program, funded by the Department of Justice. When they did their field work, I got constant calls from Southern California law enforcement, checking to be sure they were legitimate because when they entered their names, their past rap sheets would fill a room. So, with one murderer, two robbers, several social scientists, and police officers, we designed the Robbery and Violence Prevention Program. It was started in 7-Elevens, and then other convenience stores, but is now used on a widespread basis, around the country and world. In Belize, a few years ago, I saw a sign at a petrol station stating "Use low cash", which was our prototype sign designed over 30 years ago. That made me feel good. I had my own Las Vegas stories to tell at that time, as a card counter.

A college friend once said to me: "Can't you just do something as a hobby for once?" I can't. I am used to hard work, whether I am working or playing, so while working at WBSI, in the 1960s, when I was in my mid-twenties, I became a card counter in Black Jack at the tables in Las Vegas.

My Card Counting Days

Card counting went along with my statistical interest and not ever doing anything just as a hobby or leisure. The book *Beat the Dealer* had just come out, and I immediately learned "the system".[2] It had pull-out flash cards that I carried everywhere with me, and when I had a free moment, I would study my *Beat the Dealer* flash cards. You have to be statistically inclined and interested enough to do this because it is very hard work and takes a tremendous amount of concentration. In addition to counting every card, you have to change your card playing strategy according to the count of the deck. Bud, being a psychologist and statistician, would play too. He was much more interested in smoking and drinking Scotch, though, and talking with the dealer and table-mates, than he was in counting cards; so he would just watch my betting strategy to determine when he should "bet up" to take advantage of the deck because it was more favorable to the player, depending upon which cards had been played. I concentrated on counting cards and struck up no extraneous conversations with the other players or the dealer. I would count cards for 13 to 14 hours at a time, into the early morning hours, when the maintenance people started cleaning the casino around your feet.

Bud and I played Black Jack several times a year in Las Vegas for about 20 years. In the early years, we would jump in my 1965 white Mustang, with our best friends, a black couple also from San Diego, and drive to Vegas after work on Friday. We'd stay up all night, sleep a few hours in the daytime, stay up all night again on Saturday night, and then drive back taking turns driving. We were completely exhausted on Sunday night. Bud and I both worked at WBSI at that time, and we would have to go to work the next morning, but he had become the Director and my boss, so there was no one to answer to.

This was in the early days of card counting, and the casinos were just catching on. Now, there is a movie about card counting called *Twenty-One*. In that movie, they actually cheat by giving hand signals, but card counting itself is neither cheating nor illegal. To this day, it is not illegal to count cards, but the casino can make the player leave, which is what happened to me. I was kicked out (escorted) of three of the largest casinos on the Las Vegas Strip. I would make a lot of money card counting, which Bud would then immediately lose shooting craps. One night, in the late 1980s, I just scooped up my winnings and took them to a high-end shop in the casino and bought a thousand dollar brown leather jacket, which I still wear with pride and as a fond reminder of my "card counting" days.

I stopped playing Black Jack and counting cards after Bud died in 1989, and I have never played again. Now, they treat card counters differently. In my legal cases, I have seen the padded cells where they hold them, take their pictures, and send the pictures to the other casinos. In fact, I have defended a lot of the casinos all over the country in legal cases, and I walk right past the Black Jack tables and never look back.

In a recent bar fight case, which I was defending in Seattle, I was being deposed as an expert witness. On a break during my deposition, my female attorney overheard the three male attorneys on the other side say: "What would a nice lady like that know about bar fights'? I thought to myself: "I know".

CHAPTER THREE

~

ATHENA

In 1979, after working a little over thirteen years at the Institute, Bud and I left the Institute to form our own company, and I became the President of Athena Research Corporation. He insisted I become President because he had already been a President and Director. That is the way he was. Bud was a Ph.D. in Social Psychology and had founded the Institute in 1959 with another psychologist. Bud had hired me for my job initially at WBSI, in 1966, and we married in 1969. Our work together at Athena during the 1980s focused on research and consulting on crime and terrorism. In 1989, Bud died, from lung cancer, only six weeks after his diagnosis. While he was in ICU in the Scripps Hospital in La Jolla, CA, the last couple of weeks of his life, he continued working on reviewing an article for a journal, saying" "This is a professional commitment, honey. I told them I would review this article." And he did.

I had very little time or opportunity for grieving because I had to continue our company and maintain our contracts, so I continued the research alone, that he and I had started together. We had named our company *Athena* because she is, after all, the Greek Goddess of wisdom and war. Thus, our motto is: *If wisdom fails; war prevails.* The Athena Maxims, which have evolved over the years are these:

Maxims of Athena

❖ What lessons have we learned?
❖ Let's write this down.
❖ You must think at all times.
❖ Work with me on this.
❖ This is not a difficult concept.
❖ Listen and remember.
❖ We cannot be all things to all people.
❖ We cannot be wrong.
❖ Make no promises and tell no lies.

Decades of doing the research, consulting, training, presentations, videos, print media, and TV interviews led to my expertise in security and crime prevention. Talking to robbers for their ideas on robbery prevention was a big part of the research for decades. The first study was conducted at the Western Behavioral Sciences Institute (WBSI) carried out in the 1970s.[3] That research, directed by Dr. W. J. Crow, which I coordinated, was funded by the National Institute of Justice (NIJ), Law Enforcement and Assistance Administration (LEAA). For the study, 7-Elevens were used as experimental and control sites to test out what were then new ideas in crime deterrence, and the ideas came from police, social scientists and ex-robbers. The rationale of the experiment was based on the need to make the target (stores) less attractive by reducing the cash and maximizing the take\risk ratio. That is, to make the amount of money available small and the relative risk high.

The results supported the concept that robbers do in fact select their targets, and that physical and behavioral changes at the site can significantly reduce robberies. What remained to be seen was whether the results of the experiment could be applied successfully, on a large scale, over time. The program was subsequently implemented in 7-Eleven stores nationwide in 1976. After twelve years, from 1974 to 1986, robberies in 7-Elevens had decreased by nearly 65% (Crow, Erickson & Scott, 1987).[4] The concept of the program was adopted in 1987 by the National Association of Convenience Stores (NACS) for use in stores nationwide.

Most people know the results of that research from seeing the height strip markers at the entrance and exit doors in convenience stores. They are there to measure the height of the robber as he leaves the store, or later to see it on the camera. It also includes the signage about not cashing large bills; clerk cannot open safe; and maintaining low levels of cash.

Ten years after the original study, in an effort to update the findings, the Southland Corporation, operator and franchisor of 7-Eleven stores, supported the Athena Research Corporation to conduct a study of incarcerated armed robbers in five state prisons in 1985. I later designed the adult prison study in 1995 and the juvenile prison study in 2001.[5] The part that Arnie would play in that research--both personal and professional--is my next story.

CHAPTER THREE: ATHENA

CHAPTER FOUR

~

ARNIE

Certainly, who and what we become is formed by a combination of genetics and environment, including where we live, our education, whom we know, whom we marry, and what we do for a profession. Marrying my first husband, Bud Crow, was one of those lifetime choices that sets a path. Marrying Arnie Stenseth, my second husband, in 1990 was also a life-changing experience. Below, I tell what I know from Arnie's experience with child abuse in the decades when nothing like that was talked about, so no one knew. Here is just a snippet of what his life was like as a child in Sioux Falls, South Dakota in 1944, and how he survived and thrived, in spite of it all.

Arnie, at age 7, stands in the closet of his bedroom as straight and tall as the soldier he would later become. He was looking straight ahead at the closet door. His little brother John, 19 months younger, tries to stand as straight as his big brother, and he tries not to cry. They each have a bar of Lifebuoy soap in their mouths, not for the first time. Under the door, they can see the toes of their father's large black Florsheim dress shoes. Arnie is waiting for the moment, when his father will suddenly throw open the door and make sure that they are still both standing there, with the bars of soap in their mouth. If they don't, they will be beaten, which is usually the outcome anyway.

Arnie's father, a Norwegian Lutheran minister, is as tall as a barn and as harsh as a Nazi. He is wearing a white collar ruff, even off-church duty, as they did in the old country. Now, he is punishing his boys because they have been "bad boys'. How bad could they have been at 5 and 7? Despite his abusive upbringing from his father, Arnie had a strong Mother, who saved him. She served as his role model and saved his life, literally and figuratively, as did his acting later on. With acting, he would say: "I always felt I could get away and be someone else". A short chronicle of Arnie's life is the best way to put it in perspective and understand why we play and work together so well—always learning from each other. The artist and scientist, the yin and the yang. His two daughters had been asking him for years to write a chronology because they could not keep it straight. What better place to do that than in Verona, Italy, where he had once lived, and we were visiting together in 2004, shown below.

Arnie's Chronology
1937 - Born in Tyler, MN and lived in Ruthton, MN. Dad (Sigwart Stenseth) was a minister 56 years old, who had emigrated from Norway. Mom (Ruth Sorlie) was a professor of German at Augustana, 34 years old. She emigrated from Norway.
She commuted by train to Sioux Falls, South Dakota. Esther Marquardt, who spoke only German) was their live-in nanny.
1939 – 18 months later, John was born. Vi lived with the family in Ruthton. She was nine years older than Arnie. She was Sigwart's daughter, but with a different mother. Sigwart had two prior wives, both of whom died of tuberculosis. He had Vi with one, and Muriel, the older daughter, with the other. He had also lost a daughter, Dorcas, through a drowning.
1941 – The family moved to a house in Sioux Falls on 1606 Duluth Avenue and purchased it for $5,000.00, which was never paid off.
1942 – Arnie started kindergarten at Mark Twain. His father was a fill-in pastor during the war, and his mom kept teaching.
1945 – His dad had a mental breakdown, lost his hearing, and could no longer preach. He was, in Arnie's word, "deaf as a door". There was no disability or retirement from the church.
1946 – Vi left home.
1950 – Arnie graduates Mark Twain and went to Washington High School.
1952 – His mom gets a Fulbright Scholarship to Elverum, Norway for one year. The whole family crosses the Atlantic on the Queen Mary, landing in South Hampton, England. Arnie had finished his freshman year at Washington High, and had to leave his classmates. His year in Norway did not count toward high school credits, even though he went to high school in Elverum.
1953 – On Easter, Arnie, at 15, ran away from his parents in Oslo and took the train to Rome. His aunts found him in the plaza there on Easter morning. In June, his mother sent him home from Norway on an ocean liner alone to live with a chemistry professor at Augie. In fall of 1953, he returned to Washington High as a sophomore instead of a junior. He

went for three more years. The family was reunited, and his "father was crazier than ever".
1955 – In the fall, Arnie started classes at Augie while still at WHS and moved into Solberg Hall on Campus. In June, he joined the Marine Corps Reserve, going one weekend a month, and two weeks in the summer.
1956 – Arnie graduates from Washington High in January. In the spring, he started at Augie full-time. In summer, Arnie went to Camp LeJeune, North Carolina for Marine summer camp. In the fall, he went to Augustana College *again*.
1957 – Summer, he worked grain bins in the Midwest. In October, he joined the Army, and trained at Colorado Springs, CO at Camp Carson.
1958 – In January, he went to Fort Holabird, U.S. Military Intelligence Training Center in Baltimore for six months. In June, he was assigned to Southern European Task Force, SETAF, in Verona, Italy.. Member analyst with the 163rd Military Intelligence Batallion. He was 21
1960 – In the summer, he returned to the U.S. and went home to Sioux Falls.
In the fall, he returned to Augie (the same time Rosemary started, but he was five years older). He became a Democrat, whereas he had been a Republican before.
1962 – Summer stock at the Barn Theatre in Augusta, Michigan. Still attending Augie. Award Union cards for SAG-AFTRA and Actors Equity Association.
Christmas, dropped out of Augie and moved to New York to pursue acting until June, 1963.
1963 – In NY, and then summer stock at the Barn Theatre in Augusta, Michigan. He marries and has a daughter. The family moves to Sioux Falls where Arnie works as a DJ (Jerry Arnold) at KELO.
1964 – Arnie goes back to Augie, drives an Augie bus, and works at KELO.
Summer; theater in Okoboji. His mother dies in August at the age of 61.
1965 – Summer; The Fantastiks in Sioux Falls.
1966 – Spring; A.S. graduates from Augie. Summer in Okoboji.
Fall; moves to Michigan and teaches high school English for one year.
1967 – February 28, Arnie's second daughter is born. Summer; move to Vermillion and start grad school on GI bill.
1968 – Fall; USD Springfield, taught theatre for one year.
1969 – January; Arnie's dad dies at age 88 (Born in 1881). May; the

family moves to Hollywood. Studios are folding, and Arnie drops out of grad school.
1971 – Fall; Moves to Sioux Falls to become Community Playhouse directorship, and work as a DJ at KSOO as Arnie Stenseth. Arnie is 34.
1972 – May; After one season at the Playhouse, the family moves to Pierre for Arnie to become State Arts Director and work in Travel Division, PR, until Fall, when he becomes Bicentennial Director, four years before the Bicentennial.
1977-1978 – Worked as State Railroad Director for South Dakota.
1972-1979 – Lived in Pierre
1979 – October; Arnie moves to Sioux Falls and works for Kearns Machinery in advertising.
1980 – May; Divorced. October; Lost Kearns job due to a company downsizing.
1980-1989 – Lived on Whidbey Island and Everett, WA, doing acting, real estate, and job development with Operation Improvement (from 1982-1986).
1988 – Arnie is cast in the pilot movie of *Twin Peaks* as a Norwegian, which was not a stretch, since he is Norwegian and speaks the language.
1989 – Summer; Went to Sioux Falls for one year to act at Augie and Community Playhouse.
1990 – April; Arnie meets Rosie. August; Arnie moves to Seattle. On November 10, Arnie and Rosie get married and move to Georgetown.
1990-1993 – Arnie and Rosie live in Georgetown, while Arnie does theatre, film and industrials. RJ gets a Ph.D. and works full-time with Athena. Arnie becomes a CPP (Certified Protection Professional) and works with Athena.
1993 – May; Arnie and Rosie buy their first house together and move to Seattle. Arnie acts in theater and does "Bill Nye the Science Guy" and works for Athena doing prison studies.
1998 – February; Arnie and Rosie move to San Diego to 28th Street. Arnie gives up acting and works with Athena.
2000 - September 1, Rosemary's beloved Mother, Opal, dies at the age of 88, after a two year struggle with cancer.
2001 – August; Arnie and Rosie sell the 28th Street house by Balboa Park and move to Imperial Beach, CA.
2003 – October, Arnie and Rosie sell the Imperial Beach house and buy a house by McKennan Park in Sioux Falls, SD--a childhood dream

> come true for both of them.

> 2004 – Arnie and Rosie go to Verona. It is the first time he has been back in over 40 years since he was stationed here, and this is where we are writing this story. We don't know what happens next, but it's been a good run so far.

After this, in 2010, we moved to Coral Gables, Florida for three years; then back to our cabin at Swan Lake, South Dakota, just five miles from my family farm. This was the most peaceful *Walden Pond* portion of our lives, living there full time for four years. In winter, only ten of us would remain there because our neighbors, and the ducks and geese all went south for the winter.

Arnie's Acting Career

Arnie was well-prepared to do prison interviews when he began them for our studies because of his military intelligence training and his acting. He has done stage and screen, including the pilot of *Twin Peaks*, and several episodes of *Bill Nye the Science Guy*. Arnie says it was always intimidating to act with kids because they learn the lines more quickly and would say: "Mr. S., here's what you say . . ." He was trying to concentrate, on his lines in this one episode, when the hundred pound blood hound he was holding was trained to bolt at the word: "Chase". One of those beloved kids hollered that word. The Assistant Director later said that Arnie took off with the dog pulling him, and was four feet off the ground, when he went past the camera. The dog and Arnie ended in the pond, unharmed, and Disney Productions paid for Arnie's clothes.

His first movie stands out the most for him. He told it this way about his start in acting, when he wrote a letter to his niece a few years ago. His letter:

> I really go back when I think about those days of shooting *How the West Was Won* in the summer of 1961—my first movie, when I was 21. What an experience, more fun than artistic, but then it was all fun in those days. *Anaway*, (as my German/Russian neighbor says), my buddy and I heard that MGM was hiring extras for a film to be shot in Custer State Park, in South Dakota. So we packed

his pup-tent and a change of underwear into my Austin-Healey and headed West. They now refer to extras as 'color' or 'background'. Along with about 200 other guys, we were brought by bus out to the Park and spent the next week shooting the railroad segments of the film. I'm the 37th one from the left, swinging a pick. The highlight of the week was the buffalo stampede. My more educated friends correct me by telling me they are called 'American Bison'. My Lakota friend, Dallas Chief Eagle, however, said, 'stupid *Wasichu*, they're *Bufflo*", so that's what they are to me.

The last day of shooting, we were all sitting on the rail, eating our lunch, and an AD (assistant director), slowly walked by and picked out four of us. He asked us if we wanted more work. Stupid question! We were chosen to be stand-in/doubles for the four stars, Henry Fonda, George Peppard, Richard Widmark, and Russ Tamblyn. I was the same height, weight, and hair-color as George Peppard, so they issued me an exact duplicate of his wardrobe, and doubled my wage from $10 a day to $20. My buddy went home with the tent, but no problem, I had enough money now to get a hotel room in Rapid City and spend the next 2 weeks riding out to the Park in a bus with 30 Dakota Sioux. I learned real fast that they don't like to be called 'Native Americans'. Again, Dallas told me, 'We're *Indans*"! They called me General Custer or Wasichu (whitey). Unfortunately, MGM paid us daily, so our regular stop in the morning was the county jail, to pick up my new friends. Ten bucks bought a lot of fire-water in those days. Except for the constant threat of a scalping, it was great to get to know those guys. We were all in make-up and costume, so we were probably a sight.

How the West Was Won (HTWWW) was shot in three segments. 1) the Eastern US, 2) the Great Plains, and 3) the West. The director of the second part was George Marshall. He was a legend. He sat on a raised platform in a canvas chair and played catch with a baseball with some hapless AD who was ready to cry by the end of the day. He loved to throw the ball over her head, and watch her run down-hill to fetch it. Each shot took hours to set up for the Cinerama cameras, and I spent most of the day in the shade, sweating in my wool Cavalry Uniform.

George insisted on using his personal horse, a Tennessee Walker, flown out from LA. All the rest of the troop had to mount old Quarter and saddle horses, so look for any scenes involving the whole unit, led by me in the distance shots, and George for the close-ups riding that pansy-horse. One scene to watch for involves George riding up to my old friend Ben Black Elk, the chief. He was a wonderful person, and we got together every time I went to the Black Hills after that, when I worked for the South Dakota Governor in the '70s.

"Anaway", they raise their right hands and say 'How Kola', and Ben turns around on his horse and yells back into a gulch. I had just rehearsed the greeting with Ben for about 2 hours. Then George strutted in, mounted Twinkle Toes, and George Marshal, through an AD, called for quiet on the set. Now, a lot of money went into each shot, so each one was painstakingly prepared and rehearsed. However, the esteemed director assumed that all Native Americans could ride bare-back, (stupid Wasichu), so when Ben turned around, about 50 of Crazy Horse's people, in war-paint, pounded up on horse-back to chase George P. up the hill. Four or five reached the top of the gulch, clutching their pony's necks. George M. himself screamed "Cut". For the next two days, the MGM crew scoured western SD for every English saddle they could find. So, whenever I see this scene I tell people to look at the *Indan's* feet. They are all hanging on with their feet in the stirrups and the saddle hidden under their blanket pads.

It took three days to round up the herd of *Bufflos*. One cowboy said "it's easy to round up *Bufflos* – wherever they want to go". They finally got them into position for the shot where Henry Fonda shot a bull. They had to spike the water-hole with tranquilizer to do it. On the second day of this mess, Henry Fonda, (they called him Uncle Hank), asked me if I fished. I said: "Sure"! At that point, I would have agreed to jump out of a plane without a parachute. He said "come on". I found a Park Ranger who happened to have some fishing gear, and we took off into the woods. During the trip he said: "All I ask is that you don't ask me anything about the theatre or acting." "OK, Uncle Hank", I replied. We had a great four hours, sitting by a trout stream. Oddly enough, we did talk about acting, when he found out I was from Sioux Falls. He surprised me when he told me that Richard Widmark was raised in Sioux Falls, and that his whole Fonda family and the Brando family knew each other from their days at the Omaha Playhouse. Richard W. never came out of his trailer unless called to the set. The fishing scene in On Golden Pond, which I later acted in in Summer Stock in Michigan, brings back wonderful memories of the afternoon I spent fishing with Uncle Hank.

Another time . . . about my time hanging out at The Fat,

CHAPTER FOUR: ARNIE

Black Pussycat in Greenwich Village, in the 60s, with my buddy from high school, Bob Zimmerman, who later changed his last name to Dylan.

CHAPTER FIVE

~

DOING THE RESEARCH

When I married Arnie Stenseth in 1990, he and I continued my work with Athena. He had been an actor all his life, but then also took the training and testing and became a CPP (Certified Protection Professional) so that he could work with me. His work in the Army in Military Intelligence prepared him for our research, especially interviewing robbers in prison. He had a lot of good advice for me from the very beginning of our marriage.

- Don't worry about things you can't do anything about.
- Do what you do best.
- Stick with what you know.
- Find your center before making a presentation or testifying.
- Make an entrance, make an exit, and while you're there, make a difference.
- Leave them wanting more.
- Don't be around people that aren't nice to you.
- Don't be too nice, or people will take advantage of you.
- Don't take things personally.
- Be strong and tough.
- Don't overthink everything.
- Remember you're the best.
- Stand tall and sit up straight.

The last one was the most important, especially going into my first trial as an expert witness, just two years after we were married.

Each decade, I updated the research on robbers. Robbers on our WBSI staff gave us the ideas for our original robbery study in the 70s. Then, Bud and I conducted a study of prisoners to update the study in 1985. Arnie and I did the same in 1995, and then we focused on teenage robbers in 2001. We studied what robbers look for, why they do it, and what would keep them from it. The research is published in *Armed Robbers and Their Crimes* and in the *Teenage Robber Study*.[6]

Talking to teenage robbers about how to prevent robberies had not been done in this way before, and the findings of this study had not been previously published. Virtually all (85%) of the robbers from 13 to 18 years of age incarcerated in Texas in the summer of 2001 were included in the study. The juvenile robbers told us what they look for, why they do it, how they do it, and why people get hurt. They told us what they think made them violent. They gladly shared their stories because as one robber put it: "I'm so glad to be talking about robbery instead of self-esteem".

Arnie did a lot of the interviewing and surveys of the robbers nationwide and would say that upon his arrival at home, I would first ask for the data and then ask for a hug. I am glad that he understands how I am about data. I just love it.

Juvenile Prison Survey

Though we have surveyed nearly 1,000 prisoners, seeing the juvenile prisoners, in 2001 in Texas, made the biggest impression on Arnie, and he wrote about that experience and referred to them as "kids", below:

> There are four phases that all kids go through in the Texas Juvenile Prison System. They have to complete all phases. Kids must be released from the system at the age of 21. If all four phases are not completed, the kids can be kept longer. Socialization and education are goals of the whole system.
>
> 0's and 1's wear orange scrubs – cotton pants with elastic waist, orange short sleeve shirt, white t-shirt, and black high-top Converse shoes. They have to be laced. Very short laces or no laces at all mean they are on suicide watch. Phase 2 they get to take off the orange top. They have the orange pants and a gray or white t-shirt. Phase 3 they get to take off the orange pants, and they wear jeans. Phase 4 they wear jeans, short sleeved polo shirt, and black shoes. The phases are sort of an ego thing, they take pride in it. The older ones don't let the younger ones get away with anything. Seems to work. Blue represents Texas A&M – top color. Baylor next. Then green – Texas Tech. Orange represents university of Texas at the bottom.

Every institution has a unit called "Security" which is basically solitary confinement. It's a 6x10 foot steel room – walls, ceiling, floor. Bunk bed built into the wall. No showers throughout any of the units. A light in the ceiling that is covered with Bullet-Resistant Barrier (BRB) is never turned off.

Our survey was available in Spanish as well as English, as was the consent form. One juvenile at Marlin was unable to read, and was assisted by a Juvenile Correction Officer (JCO.)

JCOs were always present in the room during survey.

At all institutions, pencils were counted at the conclusion of the survey.

At all institutions, I, along with our other two interviewers, were called "sir" by the kids.

At all institutions, except Marlin, kids have 15 minutes for meals. At Marlin, it's 8 minutes. When time is up, whistle blows and the kids stand.

At each institution, kids were asked if their fathers and/or mothers have ever been incarcerated. Secondly, kids were asked if their siblings had been incarcerated. Kids were asked to write it down on the back of the last page of the survey.

It was up to each superintendent whether to participate in the study. We were lucky that they all agreed. No negative comments were made to me about the study. Guards expressed great interest in seeing the results of the study. I gave our book – *Armed Robbers and their Crimes* to each facility – one for the warden and one for the contact person with whom I met.

Kids were invited to stay afterwards, but it wasn't possible in most places because they were moved as a unit, and there weren't enough JCOs. Some did though, and I interviewed them.

All JCOs were in street clothes. No guards. No one was armed. Everyone has radios.

Three kids requested Spanish surveys.

I was struck by how young the kids were, and they all seemed scared. I didn't experience any of the belligerence that I did with the adults.

They are constantly being told to tuck in their orange scrubs and pull up their pants.

Brownwood – in Brownwood, TX (Sample 20, 17 surveyed, 85% participation) there were three of us doing the survey. Done in chapel. Kids seated in school chairs, no talking amongst the kids. Built in 1972 as a women's prison. Typical high security –

chain link fence with razor wire, 30 ft. halogen lights, no guard towers. Announce that you have an appointment. They keep your driver's license. You get a badge. You go through metal detectors, but no searches. A female officer escorted the kids to the chapel. Open campus. Every juvenile was accompanied at all times. Ratio at facilities of about 1:1 (inmate to staff).

Juveniles standing in a single line at the door at 9:00, on time. Discipline seems to be regulated by the superintendent of each institution. At Brownwood, they march double-file everywhere they go on campus, hands behind their backs with palms out and thumbs up. All heads shaved nearly bald.

Brownwood has evolved into the sexual offender facility. Usually molestation of a sibling in the home. Can be street rape.

I introduced myself and fellow researchers. JCO would have the kids sit quietly. Usually some stragglers who were in a late breakfast or lunch, or the infirmary. Gave intro as to what we were doing. Quite a few of the kids were excited when they were told the topic was robbery, so they "lit" up" when they found out it wasn't a self-esteem evaluation. The kids are constantly being evaluated for release.

San Saba – in San Saba, Texas (26 Sample, 22 participated, 85% participation) Survey administered in the cafeteria. Selected three kids each day to help in cafeteria. Some are interested in food service careers. Not an official program. Kids live in "dorms". Iron doors that clanged. A dorm holds 24-30 bunks. All beds made military-style. Each had a footlocker. No personal possessions are allowed. Place for a toilet area separated only by a low wall from the living area. Two or three urinals. No privacy. Kids must request toilet paper. (Maximum of 5 sheets). In each dorm, there is a JCO enclosed in a BRB room. Kids are watched 24 hours a day. Smell that hits in every dorm is a mixture of chemicals and urine.

Just before the survey started, JCOs jumped in, handcuffed a kid, and took him away. No idea why. Two kids refused to participate, so they sat quietly during the survey.

Three kids stayed after the survey, and talked for about 20 minutes to the interviewers.

Hamilton – in Bryan, Texas (21 sample, 19 participated, 90% participation) Superintendent wants 15 books for a class.

Survey was done in a school structure in a classroom. Fairly general population.

Lined the kids up in the hallway and did a shoelace check. Kids communicate by lacing and tying shoelaces differently. Had laces taken away from them.

One kid was in security, and the JCO offered to go get him, but I declined.

McLennan – Mart, Texas (28 Sample, 21 participated, 75% participation). Superintendent took us around. Superintendent has been in system since 1974.

Mart has section on anger management, so there are a lot of outbursts. Superintendent said that this was the calmest session he had seen in a while.

One kid – problem with anger management, 12 years old. In for taking an unlocked padlock off a door, and hitting a JCO and knocking him out.

One kid – gangly Caucasian, geeky glasses, finished test in seven or eight minutes. 15 years old. His father took a new wife when the kid was six years old, and the new wife kicked the kid out. He basically lived in the woods. Once in a while his father would let him in to shower. Met Indian in the woods who helped him build a hut. Kid loved school, so he spent time there and at the library. Extremely bright kid. Tried to help his mother out with odd jobs, pawned his bike, etc. Finally, robbed a guy of $100 at an ATM, kid arrested at the library. Mart will have 300 new single-occupancy cells.

Marlin – in Marlin, Texas (23 sample, 23 participated, 100% participation). An intake and assessment facility for the state. Every kid starts at Marlin. Met with the director, and he said that when the facility was built two years ago, the goal was to have the kids feel like they were behind bars at all times. Every door clangs shut.

Upon arrival, go into a waiting room where they take off all clothes, jewelry, possessions, etc. Those things go back with policeman who brought them to be given to the family. Metal room with benches around the edges. Kids are fingerprinted, shaved, given orange uniforms and tennis shoes, and showered with a chemical for lice removal. Kids are given complete mental evaluations: socialization, English language, emotional needs, etc. Staff of three R.N.s per shift and doctors – complete physical examinations, eye exams, and dental exams.

Marlin is an intake center.

When kids leave, they have a uniform and a bible.

Survey done in portable classroom on the campus, a little way from the administration building. Kids sat in desk chairs.

Kids march in two's, with heads down. When finished with survey, they handed it to the JCO, and were then told to put their heads down on their arms on the desks.

High security. No movement on campus.

Jefferson – in Beaumont, TX (24 sample, 16 surveyed, 67% participation). Three kids were on warrant, other four declined.

Beautiful campus, brick buildings. It sits in a complex of prisons, central of which is a federal prison. Accompanied around by a female JCO, and the kids loved her. One Hispanic kid struggled with reading the survey and held the group up a bit. General facility. No special types of treatment.

Total of six units surveyed (142 sample, 118 surveyed, 83% participation). [End Arnie's report]

Here is what Arnie wrote in a somewhat fictionalized narrative about the life of one of the young men, Errol, whom he interviewed, and it represents so many others in the same or similar situations.

A fifteen year old girl was breathing in pain, giving birth to a healthy little black boy. The only other person in the room was her grandmother, sitting at the foot of the dirty stained mattress. Real beds were not common in the row houses on East Baltimore Street.

"Sherize, honey, his name gonna be Erroll, just like my Pa" said the slight, light-colored black lady. As she changed towels and tended to the baby, Sherise shot back: "Fuck that shit. I don't give a fuck what that little shit call hisself. He on his own now, as far I am concerned".

The woman finished cleaning him off and wrapped him in her own blanket. "Don't you worry none, 'lil Erroll. Your mama don't know who your daddy is, so I'm gonna give you my daddy's old family name of Coarvey. I'll be takin' care of you anyway from now on, and you're gonna be a fine boy. Ain't that right, Cherise?"

"Whatever, Gramma. You can do whatever the fuck you want to—what you naming him again? Erroll? Good luck to both of you."

Errol lived a decent life, by some standards, until Grandma

Carrey got sick and died. Grandma had always had food ready for him when he came home from school. She washed and even ironed his t-shirts. He was a dude even though he was the littlest one. And he was smart. His teacher said so. He listened to the older guys every night when they all sat out on the stoops of their Baltimore row-houses.

One night Rabbit, counta he so fast, came up all out of breath. "Shit man, some dude just wasted that rag-head at the c-store."

"He dead?" said Errol.

"Naw, he just took him down, didn't take him out. Motherfucker not gonna be walkin' easy no time soon."

"What you got there, Rabbit?"

"The dude that shot the rag-head dropped it running out the store. I scooped it up, gonna sell it on the street."

"Damn, I wish I could buy it."

"What the fuck you gonna do with a gun? You ain't even about to see over the counter."

"I wanna take somebody out sometime. Everybody always picking on me."

"You dumb fuck. You don't take nobody out, you wanna take 'em down."

"What's the difference?"

"Out is out man – he be dead. Cops hunt you down like a rat. Down is just that, just hit 'em in the leg or arm or something. You don't wanna kill 'em man. You be servin' hard time "you take 'em out."

After his grandma's death, Errol had nowhere to go, no one to tell him he'd be alright after getting beat up. Gangs didn't even want him. So he did the best he could starting with shop-lifting, some vehicle theft, breaking and entering businesses warehouses, but still wary of confronting "the man" with a house invasion or a robbery.

His life changed again the night he got a gun. The feeling of power it gave him was overwhelming. It was just an old .22 caliber, but he knew that he needed a better one soon.

That chance came soon enough and in an unexpected way. He was sitting beside a dumpster in an alley, aiming his .22 and imagining holding up a c-store or a fast-food, maybe that McDonald's.

Suddenly he heard a noise in front of the dumpster. It was Dog Face, on account of his face getting all fucked up by some

MS 13's. "Damn they're good with their knives."

Anyway, as Dog Face stuck his ugly face around the corner, he said: "Bolo, is that you hidin' back there in the corner? Come on out here and gimme your money you little shit or I blow your head off." Damn, he be waving around a big ole 9MM Glock acting like he some hot nigger on the block. Thing is, in that dark corner he didn't see me holding my .22, so I shot him in his ugly eye. Well, I traded my little gun for a big one in that transaction. Nobody's ever gonna miss ole Dog Face and everybody knows that Little Bolo was on the other side of East Baltimore. I'm the man – I'm 12 years old and I got me a Glock – Damn!" Errol ended up in prison on another crime, and I talked to him there.

Arnie: Thanks for coming in to talk to me.
Errol: No problem.
My name is Arnie.
Whatever.
I'm doing a study on robbery. How to stop it, what a store can do to make you not want to rob it. You understand?
Yeah.
I'd like to know what you saw in the Shop-N-Go that made you think you could get away with a robbery there.
Shit, I robbed a whole bunch of stores before that one. Nothin' stopped me before. The S-N-G wasn't no different.
Do you have a street name you'd rather use?
BOLO. Police always sayin, 'be on the look-out fo that little shit'. He be BOLO again. BOLO, get it? [Be On The Lookout]
Yeah, I get it. OK BOLO. Shall we start with cameras? Did you know that there were three cameras in the Shop-N-Go?
On the street, we callin' that store S-N-G. Yeah, I knew they had cameras. They probably old, no tape, not turned on, whatever. That old man, sitting in his glass room not too smart about cameras and stuff. Anyway, so many niggers comin' in there all night, they don't know me from any other dude. Just smaller. Cain't see me out that bullet-proof-glass room anyway, so much shit on the window.
We call that 'glass room' BRB, bullet resistant barrier. Have you ever heard of that?
Yeah, I heard about it. I know my little '25 ain't going to make a hole in it, so I ain't worried. I ain't gonna shoot him that way anyway.
Did you know if he had an alarm button under the counter?

Shit, he pushing that all the time. Nobody coming.

How do you know so much about the store?

Hell, I grew up in that store. I been stealing candy and shit from that store since I was little.

Did you ever get caught?

No. He had a good suspicion that I had shit in my pockets, but he never caught me.

So you had a pretty good idea how Mr. & Mrs. Park ran that store?

Oh yeah.

Did you know how much money they had in their register?

No, but I knew it wasn't much.

How did you know that?

Cause when he get too much in it, he's putting it in a box under the counter.

So how much did you get?

From both?

Right, from the cash register and the box.

The register didn't have but thirty, thirty-five in it, but the box had over three hundred, so I took it all.

OK, BOLO, let me ask you this. How did you get Mr. Park to come out of his BRB?

Well, the man gotta come out sometime to take a pee, right? Only he must be peein' in a 40 back there, cause he never be coming out for that.

So, how did you get him?

While he be back in there, peeing in his bottle, he got his wife out stocking the shelves, so I just go in when she be filling the cooler. I just showed her the gun and brought her to the front of the store. What the man gonna do? He unlock the door and put his hands in the air, and come out.

What did you do next? Why did you shoot them?

Shit man. They can ID me. They know me.

Did they fight back?

I didn't give them time to think about that. I was only 13, man. He could've beat the shit out of me. I made them kneel down, and I shot them both in the head. I took the money from the register, and I emptied the box too, in a plastic bag. Got about three hundred fifty bucks.

Then what?

What you mean-then what? I ran to where I been staying, with my cousin.

Did anyone see you in the store, other customers?

No, an old lady was leaving the store when I come out, but she didn't pay me no mind. I was lucky.

You sure were. So, how did you get caught?

The old couple, killing and all, made such a big deal in the hood and on the TV, my cousin baby-mama got scared and called Crime-Stoppers on me.

How old are you now, BOLO?

Fifteen.

And when you turn eighteen you transfer out of juvie?

Oh, yeah. I got another hard-forty yet to go.

That's forty years without the possibility of parole, right?

You got it. And I ain't about to ask for parole then. I don't want to go back out on the street when I'm fifty-fuckin-eight years old. They shoulda just give me life. I don't give a shit.

Let me ask you this. What would have kept you from robbing the Park's store?

Shit man – you a funny dude. Ain't nothing going keep us outta that store. When he was being led out of the room, back to his cell, he turned back toward me and said: "I don't care what you do, man. I'm gonna get you".

Bye, Bolo, and good luck in 2050.

CHAPTER SIX

~

GETTING THE PH.D.

In 1994, I received a Ph.D. in Sociology: Justice from the American University in Washington, D. C. This degree combined my interest in sociology and its intersection with crime and the criminal justice system. When I applied for the program, the Department of Sociology Chair said "Why do you want your Ph.D.? You're already doing what we would like to do and making more money than we are teaching." I said: "It's important for my own self-satisfaction. My husband Bud always said I did not need a Ph. D. because he had one for both of us. I need to do this for my work in research and consulting". What I did not know is that I would begin shortly doing expert witnessing, in addition to research, training, and consulting, and it would be critical for that for qualifying as an expert in my field.

I also got my Ph.D. out of self-defense because when Arnie and I moved to Georgetown in 1990, he immediately began acting on stage, which left me alone in the evenings. I am not used to being alone, especially at night. Arnie found the Ph.D. program for me at the American University in WDC, which was in Sociology: Justice, combining both of my interests, and which would lead to my being a forensic sociologist.

When I was selecting my dissertation topic, my dissertation advisor at American University said "Why don't you just write about robbery prevention, instead of the Supreme Court? That's the research you have always done." My reply was: "I want to learn about something new and write about that". He just shook his head and said nothing more about it. He did later tell Arnie that his favorite thing about me was that, "She cuts through the bull----". That characteristic has helped me immensely in both my personal and professional life.

My dissertation and subsequent book, co-authored with Dr. Rita Simon, is on the topic of social science and the law.[7] In my dissertation, I derived a chart that connotes the differing views of the law and social science, which is so important for me when looking at cases, whether criminal or civil. That figure is shown below.[8]

Figure 1: General Characterizations of the Law and Social Science

Law	Social Science
Control of human behavior	Understanding of human behavior
Specific prediction	General prediction
Specific causation	General causation
Normative (what should be)	Positive (what is)
Laws	Norms
Irrational	Rational
Prescriptive	Value-free
Dynamic	Passive
Process-oriented	Goal-oriented
Utilitarian	Non-utilitarian
Adversarial	Cooperative
Closed	Open-ended
Limited	Continuous
Inflexible	Flexible
Individual	Generalities
Single case	Group data
Concrete	Abstract
Specific	General
Idiographic	Nomothetic
Deductive	Inductive
Definite	Tentative
Non-probabilistic	Probabilistic
Factual truth-definite	Truth-indefinite
Not objective, valid or neutral	Objective, valid & neutral
Precedent and hierarchy	Data and observation
Conservative	Liberal
Status quo	Innovative
Constant	Variable
Elected or appointed	Not elected or appointed

The figure above exemplifies the differences between the law and social science. The figure below is useful in understanding the difference between liberals and conservatives. World views are much deeper and entrenched than political differences. I used the figure to help my students understand social problems and how difficult they are to solve. In the words of Rodney King, after his police beating and six days of rioting in LA in 1992: "Why can't we all just get along?"[9] The answer is "differing world views".

Figure 2: World Views[10]

TRAGIC VISION (Conservative)	UTOPIAN VISION (Liberal)
Humans are inherently limited in knowledge, wisdom, and virtue, and all social arrangements must acknowledge those limits. (287)	We should not allow current social arrangements to restrict us from what is possible in a better world. (287)
Our moral sentiments, no matter how beneficent, overlie a deeper bedrock of selfishness. (288)	
Human nature has not changed. (288)	Human nature changes with social circumstances, so traditional institutions have no inherent value. (289)
We should distrust any formula for changing society from the top down. (289)	
We should not aim to solve social problems like crime or poverty because in a world of competing individuals, one person's gain may be another person's loss. The best we can hope for are incremental changes. (289)	

TRAGIC VISION (Conservative)	UTOPIAN VISION (Liberal)
Solutions to social problems are elusive. (292)	Solutions to social problems are readily available. (292)
War is rational and a strategy for people to gain something for themselves or their nation. (292)	War is a pathology that arises from misunderstandings, shortsightedness, and irrational passions. (292)
The only way to ensure peace is to raise the cost of war to potential aggressors by developing weaponry, arousing patriotism, rewarding bravery, flaunting one's might and resolve, and negotiating from strength to deter blackmail. (293)	War is to be prevented by public expressions of pacifism, better communication, less saber-rattling, fewer weapons, less emphasis on patriotism, and negotiation. (292)
Crime is inherently rational, so the most effective crime prevention program is rational incentives, like punishment. (293)	Crime is inherently irrational and should be prevented by identifying the root causes. (293)
Social programs, such as welfare, might encourage dependency. (290)	Social goals and policies should target social problems directly, like attacking poverty by the war on poverty, pollution by environmental regulations, racial imbalances by preferences, carcinogens by bans on food additives. (290)

R. J. Erickson, adapted from Steven Pinker[11]

In the 1990s, I began to serve as an expert witness in security cases for premises liability and to testify before city, state, and federal legislative bodies, including the U. S. House Committee on Crime against Small Business and the U. S. Department of Labor. For over 20 years, I consulted on workplace violence and safety with the National Institute on Occupational Safety and Health (NIOSH), the research branch of OSHA, and conducted a multi-year study with UCLA. This study was funded by NIOSH to test out our original robbery and violence prevention program in other settings.

My primary professional interest has always been sociological and criminological research, but I have also taught at two universities. I taught public policy at the American University in 1992, in Washington, D. C., and I taught Introductory Sociology and Social Problems in 2002 and 2003 at San Diego State University. My work has always included giving speeches and presentations, along with media interviews to either report on research findings, opine on criminal events and crime trends, or to train practitioners in robbery and violence prevention. The results of my research have also led to developing robbery and violence prevention programs and safety in the workplace for some of the largest companies in the country and world, and the professional associations that represent them. The most gratifying experience, in my professional career is when a clerk in a convenience store comes up to me and say, "You saved my life."

When I am sitting across from an attorney during a deposition in a civil case, I often say to myself: "Why did you get into this line of work? Why didn't you become an interior decorator where your clients love you for making their lives beautiful and happy--not a profession, where the goal of the other side is to tear you down, destroy your credibility and make everything good that you have ever done seem somehow disgraceful, meaningless, and abject, and that you yourself are an opportunistic hired gun." As an old Kentucky lawyer once told me, "Our favorite thing to do as a lawyer is to beat up on experts. Unlike other witnesses, you're being paid, so you are fair game."

I did not make a conscious decision to become an expert witness. It was just a natural evolution of over twenty years of research and experience in a very specific field that led to my expert witnessing as a forensic sociologist. Within that area of security and premises liability is a special niche, and I am the only female Ph.D. forensic sociologist who is an expert witness in security premises liability cases. In fact, I could *not* have planned it in my early career, like you could plan to be a nurse or a teacher, which was the norm in the 60s. Forensic sociology and these kinds of tort liability cases did not exist at that time.

CHAPTER SIX: GETTING THE PH.D.

I sometimes think, as I face that same attorney, maybe I should have gone into laboratory work where I would extract liquid from fava beans in order to test the amino acids for nutritional value because no one would have an opinion about that. With my career path, everyone I meet on an airplane, at a meeting, or a cocktail party has an opinion about crime. They know how to prevent it, how to solve it, and most definitely how to punish the people who do it. And since people started watching *CSI, Criminal Minds,* and other crime series and movies, the jurors themselves are ready and feel qualified, in their minds, to help solve the crime at issue in the case. For the first time in my years of expert witnessing, the jurors will actually send questions for *me*, through the Judge, while I'm on the stand. Questions will include things to consider like tests to run, research to carry out, people to interview, and DNA and blood to be tested. The jurors focus on the interesting part of my cases, which is the crime that has been committed leading to the litigation, not the leases or contracts regarding the businesses being sued.

This is how my cases work. The security premises liability cases are a result of a crime, usually a violent crime. I do not do "slip and falls". This is not about slipping on a green bean in the produce aisle of a supermarket and suing the supermarket for your injuries. My cases are a result of a criminal act of violence where someone gets hurt, raped, or killed. If they choose to sue the owner of the location, like the hotel where a woman was raped, then the victim (or the victim's estate) is represented by the plaintiff's attorney in the civil suit and the location is represented by the defense lawyer.

Civil suits often, but not always, follow the criminal suit, if the perpetrator or perpetrators have been caught. Usually both sides in the civil suit hire experts in security to testify, and expert witnesses should take both plaintiff and defense cases to show their impartiality. Expert witnesses work on a fee bases, and ethically should never work on a contingency basis. Compensation must never depend on the outcome of the case because experts should not have a vested interest in the outcome. Experts are there to give the best representation for the plaintiff or the defense, in a fair and impartial way.

Ironically, this type of litigation grew out of a case in 1983 that occurred in Sioux Falls, South Dakota, just thirty miles from where I had grown up. There, late one night, in a hospital parking structure, a young, white woman was abducted, raped, and murdered by a white male, who had just been released on parole from the state prison a few miles away. The case led to escort service for nurses (female) in hospitals when they go to their cars late at night, and it also led to security premises liability civil cases because the hospital was sued for not providing a safe environment. Twenty years later, while living in Sioux Falls, South Dakota I had a housekeeper and coincidentally, it was her sister, who had been raped and murdered.

My housekeeper could not believe that I was doing this kind of work, which she recognized from the files, depositions, and court documents that she saw on my desk. They were all too familiar to her from the suit they had filed on behalf of her sister over twenty years earlier. It was twenty-three years after the murder of her sister, but the emotional scars were as close to the surface as you would have expected a week after the event, which shows not only what the victims go through but also what their families go through, whose lives are forever changed.

In my research and writing, I always include the sex, race, and age of individuals in these cases because that is what sociologists do. We look at the demographics of individuals. At a cocktail party, expect a sociologist's first question of someone they have just met to be, "What do you do?" That is what a sociologist wants to know. A writer would want to know what books you have read. I can already tell your sex, race, and age, so the next thing on the list is what you do. Knowing that goes a long way toward understanding an individual. If it's a young person or student, I will ask what your parents do or what you are majoring in. That is just the way sociologists think. If at the same cocktail party, someone is telling a story about an event, I first want to know when it happened and where it happened because I need information to place the event in the historical and geographical context. That is just the way sociologist are. Sociologists are linear, like historians.

When watching a fantasy movie, Arnie will say to me: "Suspend belief." That is not going to happen with a sociologist. My husband is an actor, so he lives his life suspending belief. For a sociologist, people and events must be firmly planted in reality. Everything needs to be exact and accurate—that is what research is all about, and that is what science is about. It is not based on approximations or estimates, but on the evidence, facts, and truth. This makes it very closely akin to police investigations, but not as close to the law, as we will see. The differences between science and the law show through in my cases.

One wonders how we ever co-exist in these cases and in the courtroom, as scientists and lawyers, with such different world-views, perspectives, and needs. Lawyers want you as the expert to be definite; while as a scientist, you'll commonly make an argument and then follow it by saying "On the other hand." Your lawyer does not want to hear that. The lawyer wants you, as an expert witness, to keep it simple, interesting, and unequivocal. The law is black and white, while the social sciences are often gray and ever-changing. In my experience, there is no room for nuance in the law.

I want to talk about those differences between the law and social sciences, I want to talk about the horrific crimes that lead to these civil liability cases, I want to place it in historical and geographical context. Some years ago, a Southern judge, in a homicide case, called me over to the bench and said: "The problem is all these blacks coming in now, isn't it?" I assumed or hoped it was a rhetorical question and did not even try to answer it because I know better than to answer any question informally, and off the record, to a judge.

Bud and I were together, working and as a couple for 23 years, to the end of his life, when he died in 1989 at the age of 65 of lung cancer. He had been a Navy fighter pilot and had started smoking while in the service. With his death, when I was 46, my life had to start over, professionally and personally. A few days before his death, he pulled me close to him and said: "You will be okay. You know more than you think you do; you can do more than you think you can; and don't ever become an expert witness". I probably should have listened to him about expert witnessing. It is a grueling profession, where the goal of the other side is to tear down your credibility, question your credentials, and try to make you feel totally worthless. Some of my colleagues have not had good experience as experts. One of my friends left the business and sold potato skins at the Texas State Fair; another said he'd rather drive a school bus; another one went to a mental institution; another quit working witnessing entirely, and another former security expert and cop shot himself in the head, dying instantly.

CHAPTER SIX: GETTING THE PH.D.

CHAPTER SEVEN

~

WORKING THE CASES

My first trial was in 1992 in Pikeville, KY, and Arnie tells the story of the trial in this way:

> "Hey, RJ. It's time to get up."
> "I can't. I'm comatose."
> "C'mon, it's time to take your shower."
> "Comatose people can't take showers."

Covers go over her head again. She has to be in the courtroom in an hour. The drive down from Georgetown, DC to Pikeville, Kentucky, the day before, had been peaceful and relaxing, but she had been getting tense about her first trial as an expert witness. In the final leg from Abingdon, Virginia, we were reminded of the tragic pockets of poverty existing through Appalachia, with the coal mine clearing visible everywhere. We were in my Porsche 911 Cabriolet, "they" were sitting on curbsides on the main street of each town we passed through. "They" being the Appalachian children, clad in skimpy clothes with skinny arms and legs sticking out, while their parents stood in line at the multiple lung clinics in each town we went through.

Once RJ managed to get up, we sat on the edge of our bed at the Pikeville Inn, and she rattled on and on saying "I don't think I can do this. What if they are mean to me? What if I forget something about my research and data? What if the jury doesn't like me? What if I don't do a good job for my lawyer?"

I much prefer calling her RJ instead of Rose, Rosie, Rosamaria, or other derivations of Rosemary Jean Erickson. She's RJ to me. She obviously prefers to call me Arnie too, rather than my given name of Sigwart, and she kept her maiden name of Erickson and wasn't tempted to take mine—Stenseth. Now, I was about to give her the first and only comforting, encouraging talk I would need to give her over the next twenty plus years of her expert witnessing career.

"RJ, you know that you know more than anyone else in the industry about violence in convenience stores, you literally wrote the book on it. You have a super-great lawyer, and you know the facts in the case backwards and forwards. We just visited the crime site yesterday, so you are familiar with that, and you are the best, okay? You can do this."

She looked up at me with her clear Nordic blue eyes and said: "But I didn't bring the right thing to wear. I just know it." So, it turns out, she wasn't as worried about what she was going to say, as she was about what she was going to wear. Girls. I should have known, having had two daughters, that it is always about what you wear, but I just don't get that.

I'm not known for my patience, as my daughters will testify, but it was very much needed at this crucial point in time, and in RJ's career, for her first expert witnessing in front of a judge and jury. I looked down at my little blonde Ph.D. sociologist, and said "Honey, your lawyer said the fanciest dresser in the jury box has on blue jeans and a sweatshirt that says "Pikeville Jr. College", so just pick out one of your plainest outfits from the three bags you brought— lose the suits and high heels, and no bling. Wear your mother's modest wedding ring, not your 2-carat diamond wedding ring, sit up straight in the witness box, smile at the jury, and you'll be fine."

At 1 o'clock, that afternoon, after the tortuous showering, hair blowing, make-up, and five changes of clothes and shoes, we met the defense lawyer for lunch. He is our tall, young, soft-spoken, bright lawyer—the kind you want to call Counselor—and he had me sit in the back row of the courtroom, while he kept Dr. Erickson in tow for her appearance.

The case had been brought by a man who had been standing in line around 11 PM, at a C-store/gas station. For some unknown reason, the man behind him stabbed him in the back with a buck-knife. Fortunately, the victim lived. He subsequently sued the gas station in civil court for his injuries. It was a premises liability security case, which was Dr. Erickson's expertise, and he claimed that the station had inadequate security. The perpetrator was found to be mentally ill and incapable of standing trial, so he was not incarcerated and rather was running loose somewhere in the area. That did not help RJ's peace of mind either, as she approached her defense in the case of the station.

The judge invited RJ to the witness box and summoned the jury. "Ah", I thought as the jury filed in "She dressed perfectly. Now she'll be happy because she will know that too."

In this particular courtroom, the Judge's bench was quite high, as was the jury box. The witness box, on the other hand was low. The case was announced, and the judge turned to RJ and asked her to rise for the oath. She did so, but so did the entire jury. They had misunderstood the judge's instructions, and when they rose, the entire courtroom broke out in laughter. Because the jury was behind her, RJ didn't know why everyone was laughing, and thought it was something she did wrong.

Since college, where we met, RJ has maintained a pretty constant weight of 125 pounds on her 5'4" frame. She spends most of her time trying to lose the same five pounds. She counts the number of grapes she eats, so she knows how many calories. She measures her wine in a measuring cup before pouring it. She eats exactly one-half of what is on her plate in a restaurant and takes the other half home, or to her hotel room. At any rate, she looked very tiny at that moment looking up at the judge, in his long black robe, while the court reporter administered the oath to "Dr. Erickson".

Over the years, many lawyers have tried to belittle or anger little Dr. RJ at trial by refusing to address her as "Dr." for the Doctor of Philosophy degree she earned in Sociology: Justice at the American University in Washington, D.C. with Phi Beta Kappa honors. The plaintiff's attorney on the other side, however, was a very polished gentleman from Louisville, KY, determined to commit judicial hara-kiri, when he swaggered up to the jury box. He leaned casually in on his podium in front of her and addressed her as, "Little Lady". I thought to myself, "You, Counselor, are a dead man." Four hours of questioning later, he threw his clipboard down on the desk and said, "Pass the witness".

The defense attorney cleverly rested his case, so there could be no further questions. The jury gave a unanimous verdict for the defense. It was RJ's first trial, and it had ended positively. Her lawyer advised us, however, that since the perpetrator was back on the streets, and had been spotted, it might be a good idea to leave town quickly and before dark. He did not have to say that twice. We drove to Abingdon, VA and had a wonderful evening in a suite at the historic Martha Washington Inn. The two of us, having our late dinner, sat almost alone in the elegant dining room, eating duck with cranberry sauce and feeling far away from Pikeville, KY. One trial down.

Introduction to the Cases

No more being comatose for me, like I was before my first trial. From then on, it was one case after the other. I did not realize after the first trial that no two cases would ever be alike, and that is what would make my next twenty-five years of expert witnessing so interesting. Each of the next chapters presents an individual case. The basis of selection from over 200 of my cases is neither scientific, nor statistically representative, of the cases I have done or of the crimes that occur. Rather, these are the ones that struck me in a personal way because they mostly occurred in day-to-day circumstances to ordinary people. These crimes are perpetrated on individuals, who were just doing ordinary activities in ordinary places and ended up being murdered or raped—some by serial killers. They are examples of being at the wrong place at the wrong time and becoming victims of random opportunistic crimes committed by some of the most evil men in the world.

My research on criminals and my experience with legal cases involving criminal events led to the development of my model *Evolution of a Violent Event*, shown in Figure 3 below.[12] It was derived from an earlier version by Erickson & Crow in 1980. As the chart shows, the perpetrator and victim have certain psychological and social variables. The potential target can also play a role with intervening prevention variables (security measures). This is the paradigm I use in evaluating cases. Nearly all cases are also evaluated on the commonly known *Crime Prevention Through Environmental Design—CPTED*; shown below in Figure 4; and on types of workplace violence, shown in Figure 5, *The Four Types of Workplace Violence*.

Figure 3: Evolution of a Violent Event[13]

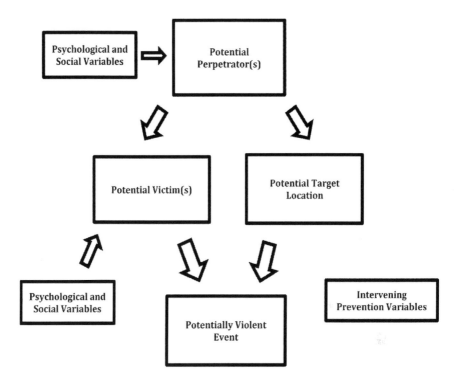

EVOLUTION OF A VIOLENT EVENT

Figure 4: Crime Prevention Through Environmental Design[14]

CPTED	
Surveillance	Involves the location and use of physical features, electrical and mechanical devices, activities, and people to maximize visibility, i.e., lighting, cameras, and clear lines of sight. Creates a risk of detection for intruders and offenders and a perception of safety for legitimate users.
Territoriality	Uses physical features and activities to express ownership and control of the environment, i.e., landscaping, signage, fencing, and border definition. Discourages presence of outsiders by delineating private and semi-private spaces, controlling the movement of people and vehicles.
Access Control	Employs people, electrical and mechanical devices, and natural measures to create a perception of risk to offenders and deny them access to targets, i.e., locks and guards.

Figure 5: Types of Workplace Violence[15]

Type 1—External—Assault or threat by outside third parties, usually criminals. No legitimate relationship with the affected workplace, which is commonly a retail establishment.
    o Examples: Robbers, Rapists, Murderers
    o 75%

Type II—Service-related—Assault or threat by someone who is the recipient of a service provider by the affected workplace, such as health care providers and the public sector, i.e., police, parole, welfare
    o Examples: Patients, Clientele,Customers
    o 15%

Type III—Internal—Assault or threat by an individual who has an employment-related involvement with the affected workplace.
    o Examples: disgruntled employees, troubled employees, management problems, co-worker problems, acquaintance problems, domestic problems
    o 5%

Type IV—Internal—Personal relationships. Assault or threat by an individual who has a personal relationship with an employee in the affected workplace.
    o Examples: domestic problems, acquaintance problems
    o 5%

Figure 6: Target Attractiveness[16]

What would be important to you if you were to rob a convenience store? Comparison of Samples

Factors	Adult Robbers Rank Order	Juvenile Robbers Rank Order
1. Escape Route	1	1
2. Amount of Money	2	2
3. Active Police Patrols	5	3
4. Anonymity	3	4
5. Armed Guards	4	5
6. Armed Clerks	6	6
7. Number of Clerks	9	7
8. Interference	7	8
9. Bullet Resistant Barriers	8	9
10. Alarm System	10	10
11. Number of Customers	11	11
12. Camera System	12	12
13. Video Recording	13	13
14. Unarmed Guards	14	14

Figure 7: Deterrence Factors[17]

Deterrence Factors	Adult Robbers Percent Deterred	Juvenile Robbers Percent Deterred
1. Bullet resistant barrier	76	82
2. Armed guard on duty	69	76
3. Frequent police patrol	63	71
4. Revolving doors	64	62
5. Armed clerk	60	61
6. Alarm system	52	65
7. Metal detector	55	51
8. Fences blocking escape	51	54
9. Longer sentences	45	53
10. Good visibility	40	54
11. Good lighting	33	44
12. Camera covering area	39	29
13. Rob before closing	28	37
14. Video camera in use	39	26

The juveniles only were asked to rate the same deterrence factors, comparing convenience stores and any location. Figures 6 and 7 show the rank-order by what they look for in the convenience store setting, and they correlate almost identically to what they would look for at *any location*, with escape route and money ranking first and second and videos and unarmed guards at the bottom of the list. The specific advice given to victims included what is shown in Figure 8.

Figure 8: Advice from Robbers to Victims to Keep from Getting Hurt

DO:	DON'T:
• Cooperate • Give up the money • Obey the robber's commands • Keep your hands in sight	• Resist • Talk • Plead • Stare • Make any sudden movements • Be a hero • Chase or follow

Figure 9 shows more of what was learned from the teenage robbers in the 2003 study and why you should fear them.

Figure 9: Teenage Robbers Survey Results

- Overall, the teenagers' selection of targets to rob and what they look for at the location is virtually identical with that of the adults.
- However, they expect much more money from any location than do the adults, and they have an escalated view of the amount of money that they are going to get.
- The most important thing they look for is escape route, followed by money. Cameras and unarmed guards, on the other hand, make little difference to them.
- They have a bravado beyond that of the adults, as far as power and control. They believe they can do virtually anything with a partner and a gun.

- They feel all-powerful if they have a gun *and* a partner, and they are more likely to have both than are the adults.
- Fully 90% did not think they would be caught and an equal number did *not* know how long their sentence would be.
- Even more than the adults, half of the teenage robbers say they were drunk or high at the time of the robbery.
- They had committed multiple robberies, even at this young age.
- They committed more violent types of robberies, including street mugging, car-jacking, and home invasions.
- Almost half wore disguises, more often than the adults.
- Half of them were members of gangs but said that is not why they committed the robbery.
- They can rob, but many can't drive because they are not old enough to be licensed. Sixty percent lived within two miles of the site they robbed, while 40% of the adults lived that close. They tell us why people get hurt in robberies.
- They tell us how victims can keep from getting hurt in robberies.
- They're most likely to rob for the money (almost half), but some do it just for the thrill and the rush.
- The neighborhood is the biggest influence on their violence. Three-fourths of them said they experienced violence in their neighborhood when they grew up.
- Three fourths of them said that that they learned to be violent from their friends.
- Nearly half of them experienced violence in their homes when they grew up.
- They were taught to be violent both by their family and friends, but most often their friends. Eighty percent of their friends commit crimes.
- Family members that coached them specifically in violence included fathers, mothers, uncles, brothers, and even grandmothers.
- Nearly half of the juvenile robbers had a parent or sibling in prison.
- They also claim that they learned to be violent from movies, television, videos and music, and they name the movies and music that influenced them.
- Three-fourths said that they had a religious upbringing, and half said they attended church regularly when they grew up.

From other research, there are both validated and un-validated security measures that emerged for robbery prevention. These are shown in Figures 10 and 11.[18]

Figure 10: Deterrence Measures – Validated

DETERRENCE MEASURES – VALIDATED

- Keeping low amounts of cash in the register
- Ensuring good visibility
- Maintaining good lighting
- Limiting access and escape routes
- Training employees in proper behavior

Figure 11: Deterrence Measures – Un-validated

DETERRENCE MEASURES – UN-VALIDATED

- Employing multiple clerks at night
- Using bullet-resistant shielding
- Employing guards or off-duty police officers at night

Cameras and video systems are not shown in either of the tables above because they have not been determined to serve as a robbery deterrent. They are, however, enjoying widespread usage. As the technology has improved, cameras and video systems have grown in popularity, and they are useful in identifying the suspect. They have essentially become state-of-the-art in the industry, even though robbers place them nearly at the bottom of the list of their considerations.

OSHA

In the early 1990s, I consulted with Federal OSHA and the convenience store industry in jointly adopting guidelines for reducing workplace violence.[19] They were issued first in 1998 and updated in 2009. A separate document was created for healthcare and social service workers and taxi drivers. Appendix A of this OSHA document is helpful in site planning and in litigation to determine if foreseeability was being assessed and if appropriate reasonable security measures were being instituted. I have included OSHA's Appendix A for reference.

Appendices

Appendix A:
Sample Workplace Violence Factors and Control Checklists

These sample checklists can help employers identify present or potential workplace violence problems. They contain various factors and controls that are commonly encountered in retail establishments.

Not all of the questions listed here fit all types of retail businesses, and these checklists obviously do not include all possible topics specific businesses need. Employers should expand, modify, and adapt these checklists to fit their own circumstances. These suggestions are not new regulations or standards, and the fact that an employer does not adopt a listed control does not prove a violation of the General Duty clause. ("N/A" stands for "not applicable").

Sample Checklist 1:

Yes	No	N/A	Environmental Factors
			Do workers exchange money with the public?
			Is the business open during evening or late-night hours?
			Is the site located in a high crime area?
			Has the site experienced a robbery in the past 3 years?
			Has the site experienced other violent acts in the past 3 years?
			Has the site experienced threats, harassment, or other abusive behavior in the past 3 years?
Yes	**No**	**N/A**	**Engineering Controls**
			Do workers have access to a telephone with an outside line?
			Are emergency telephone numbers for law enforcement, fire and medical services, and an internal contact person posted next to the phone?
			Are emergency telephone numbers programmed into company telephones?
			Is the entrance to the building easily seen from the street and free of heavy shrub growth?
			Is lighting bright in outside, parking and adjacent areas?
			Are windows and views outside and inside clear of advertising or other obstructions?
			Is the cash register in plain view of customers and police cruisers to deter robberies?
			Is there a working drop safe or time access safe to minimize cash on hand?
			Are security cameras and mirrors placed in locations that would deter robbers or provide greater security for employees?
			Are there height markers on exit doors to help witnesses provide more complete descriptions of assailants?
			Are employees protected through the use of bullet-resistant enclosures in locations with a history of robberies or assaults in a high crime area?
Yes	**No**	**N/A**	**Administrative/Work Practice Controls**
			Are there emergency procedures in place to address robberies and other acts of potential violence?
			Have workers been instructed to report suspicious persons or activities?
			Are workers trained in emergency response procedures for robberies and other crimes that may occur on the premises?

Yes	No	N/A	Administrative/Work Practice Controls (*continued*)
			Are workers trained in conflict resolution and in nonviolent response to threatening situations?
			Is cash control a key element of the establishment's violence and robbery prevention program?
			Does the site have a policy limiting the number of cash registers open during late-night hours?
			Does the site have a policy to maintain less than $50 in the cash register? (This may not be possible in stores that have lottery tickets and payouts.)
			Are signs posted notifying the public that limited cash, no drugs, and no other valuables are kept on the premises?
			Do workers have at least one other person throughout their shifts, or are other protective measures utilized when workers are working alone in locations with a history of robberies or assaults in a high crime area?
			Are there procedures in place to assure the safety of workers who open and close the store?

No site planning or litigation analysis is complete without looking at the prior crimes at the location in the area. Police Calls for Service (CFS) and police reports can be obtained for the location or for within a given radius from the police department. Depending upon the case, and whether crime in the area is an issue, I will use the CAP Index described below.

The CAP Index

The CAP Index is a sophisticated computer analysis designed to identify the risk of crime at a location.[20] The Index is used by banks, hotels, apartments, convenience stores, service stations and other businesses to assess the vulnerability of a location for crime when they are seeking to put a new business in, or if they feel that the neighborhood has changed where their business is located. Depending upon the CAP index score, they know whether they need to take extra security measures. If the score is over 100, then the vulnerability to crime is higher than average. If the score is under 100, then the vulnerability to crime is lower than average.

The Factors Measured

The CAP Index measures not only prior crimes but also the social disorganization of the neighborhood, which is another way to predict crime. The social disorganization data include education, poverty, unemployment, population mobility, and other housing and population data.

The Scores

The CAP scores are based on the risk at a location compared to the national average. A value of 100 represents the average risk of crime for the location. A score of 50 represents one-half of the average risk of crime nationwide, a score of 200 represents twice the national average, and a score of 1000 represents ten times the national average.

The Radius

The CAP score includes the crime and social disorganization within a three-mile radius. A one-mile radius is shown with the inner dotted circle, and the three mile radius is shown with the outer dotted circle. The CAP map indicates through color shading the crime vulnerability scores. Green is the lowest from 0-99, which is below average. Yellow is 100-199, which is elevated from the average. Pink is 200-399, which is two to four times the average crime vulnerability; salmon is 400-799, and red is the highest score for the CAP Index, ranging from 800 and up.

Crimes Measured

The crimes measured for the CAP Index include all violent *crimes against the person*, including rape, robbery, homicide and aggravated assault and also include *property crimes* of burglary, larceny and motor vehicle theft.

State and County Scores

The CAP Index also reports a comparison to the state and county scores, as well as the comparison to the national average.

Over Time

The CAP Index also shows the scores for years prior and years into the future. This allows trending information for whether crime has gone up or down from the past or can be expected to go up or down from the present. The map below from CAP Index is used on their website to show the CAP score for the White House (Figure 12). The crime vulnerability score for the White House in 2016 was 667, which means it is over 6 times more vulnerable than an average location in the United States, which would be a score of 100. On the right side of the chart, you will note that you can compare individual crimes, such as personal versus property crimes. Crimes against person in the area scored 533, and crimes against property were even greater at

887.

Figure 12: CAP Index

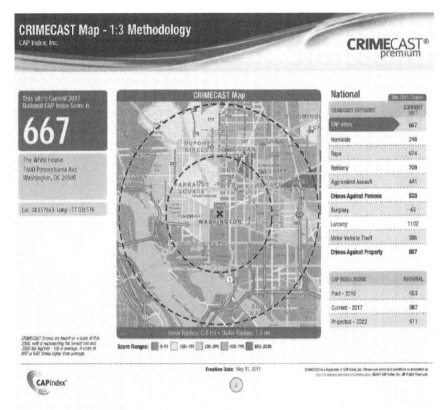

The purpose of the CAP Index in litigation is to show the crime vulnerability for the area. The purpose in site selection is to help determine what extra security measures may need to be added. After one of my trials, where the CAP map was used as a display for the jury, the judge called me over and said: "Could you get me a copy of that? I live in that area, and I want to show my neighbors". It was a good CAP score for his area. Whenever I am about to move to a new location, I order a CAP Index. I have lived in areas with a CAP Index as low as 14 (all green-rural) and as high as 365 (mostly red-urban).

Another map, shown on Figure 13 below, is a sample of where my cases may be at any one time i.e., all over the country. This one exemplifies 28 cases on August 27, 2011. It is not necessarily representative of geography because it varies over time, based on many factors, including how litigation-friendly the state laws are for this type of case. Another thing that varies over time is whether I am defense or plaintiff. When I started expert witnessing, I did mostly defense of convenience stores, but that expanded to other types of places, so that now I am one-half plaintiff and one-half defense in all sorts of venues. On this map, most of my cases were in Florida, which led us to move to Coral Gables, FL, in 2010, so I would have less travel. That also placed us nearer to the crime areas and the criminals in our cases, so the proximity was a dual-edged sword. Thus, we returned to the lake in South Dakota in 2012, with a CAP Index of 14, and we were not even on GPS.

Figure 13: Map of my Cases

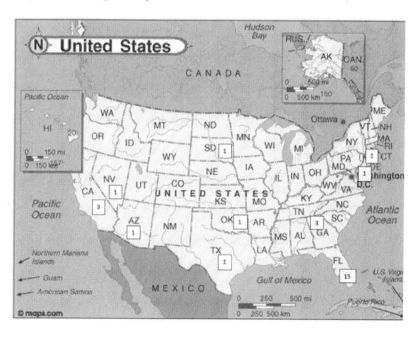

Another useful paradigm in understanding the cases to be discussed is the difference in types of murderers—serial, spree, or mass—as explained by John Douglas, FBI profiler, without his examples, on his website.[21]

Multiple Homicides
Serial Killers, Spree Slayers and Mass Murderers

People who kill more than once aren't necessarily serial killers. People sometimes mistake one kind of killer for another. You'll see a book written about a serial killer when the person was really a mass murderer. During my research into the mind of the killer, I came up with three categories to define the killing of groups of people: serial murder, spree murder and mass murder.

Serial murder

Serial murder generally involves three or more victims. The main thing that sets this category apart from the others is that there's a cooling-off period between the murders. The hiatus could be days, months or years. In other words, the serial killer isn't killing with frequency. Part of the reason for that is that the organized type of killer isn't generally a risk taker. He wants to be sure that if he decides to commit a crime, he's going to be in a win-win position. Secondly, he doesn't have to kill often if he's taking mementos. He'll have some clothing or jewelry belonging to the victim, so he'll be able to relive the crime and extend the fantasy.

A serial killer usually goes after strangers, but the victims tend to share similarities, such as gender, age or occupation. Though he prefers a certain look or background, it doesn't mean he won't substitute another victim if he can't find his intended target. It's hard to estimate, but at any given time there are between 35 and 50 serial killers in this country -- and that's a conservative estimate. About a dozen serial killers are arrested each year.

Areas where you have prostitution, a drug culture, runaways, so-called throwaways, street people and children gravitating to

---

bus depots are fertile grounds for serial killers. Compounding the problem, there are more than 17,000 police agencies in this country, some with limited technology and the inability to share information. If there's an inability to link cases, agencies may not even know they have a serial killer on their hands. Throw into the mix the mobility of the offender -- within a state or across state lines -- and he can get away with murder.

Spree murder

The next category is spree murder. Spree killers tend to do their damage within a short time span. There's generally no cooling-off period. They're like killing machines up to the point that they're caught or they turn themselves in. The killer often commits suicide or goes for what's known as suicide by cop -- putting himself in a position where police will have to kill him. Spree killers usually select victims randomly, but go for those who will meet their personal needs at the time. In other words, they'll kill for money, sex or simply because they're hungry. In cases involving spree killers, authorities usually know who they are looking for: They have the killer's identity. As a fugitive, he may go to an area where he feels comfortable. Sometimes you hear about a spree serial killer, a sort of hybrid, where there's a shorter time span involved, perhaps days, and where the victims may not have a common thread.

Mass murder

The last category is mass murder. A mass murderer kills his victims -- three or more -- at one time and in one place. While it's one event, there may be multiple crime scenes. Someone may commit a murder inside a building and then kill more people outside or down the block. These typically are the cases where there's violence in the workplace, like the shootings in post offices around the country. While this is often a mission-oriented type of crime and the killer is going after a selected or symbolic group, he'll randomly kill other people who happen to be there at the time. [End John Douglas website].

Psychopath and Sociopath

For purposes of my cases, I consider the definition of a serial killer to be the unlawful killing of two or more victims by the same offender(s) in separate events. This definition was agreed upon by the FBI Symposium members in the early 2000s. It was held on the topic *Serial Murder: Multi-Disciplinary Perspectives for Investigators*. The advantage of using two, rather than three, as the number of victims, is that the FBI can become involved in the investigation earlier.

A widely used check list of psychopathy is one advanced by Dr. Robert D. Hare. Hare's 20-item Psychopathy Check List is found below:[22]

Hare Psychopathy Checklist-Revised: 2nd Edition™
Robert D. Hare, Ph.D.

1. GLIB and SUPERFICIAL CHARM

2. GRANDIOSE SELF-WORTH

3. NEED FOR STIMULATION or PRONENESS TO BOREDOM

4. PATHOLOGICAL LYING

5. CONNING AND MANIPULATIVENESS

6. LACK OF REMORSE OR GUILT

7. SHALLOW AFFECT

8. CALLOUSNESS and LACK OF EMPATHY

9. PARASITIC LIFESTYLE

10. POOR BEHAVIORAL CONTROLS

11. PROMISCUOUS SEXUAL BEHAVIOR

---

12. EARLY BEHAVIOR PROBLEMS

13. LACK OF REALISTIC, LONG-TERM GOALS

14. IMPULSIVITY

15. IRRESPONSIBILITY

16. FAILURE TO ACCEPT RESPONSIBILITY FOR OWN ACTIONS

17. MANY SHORT-TERM MARITAL RELATIONSHIPS

18. JUVENILE DELINQUENCY

19. REVOCATION OF CONDITION RELEASE

20. CRIMINAL VERSATILITY

[End Dr. Hare's Checklist]

Psychopathy and sociopathy will be used interchangeably and discussed in relation to each of the serial killers, discussed in these four civil cases, for which I was an expert. The civil cases ebb and flow for the expert as follows, and my cases have lasted anywhere from a month to ten years. I am involved with each step of the case. Only 9 out of 10 of this kind of civil case goes to trial because the cases either settle or are dismissed.

EXPERT WITNESS CIVIL CASE PHASES
Phase 1. The attorney calls and describes the case.
Phase 2. If I agree to take the case, the attorney sends a retainer check and agreement, along with the materials to review.
Phase 3. I review the materials and request additional materials.
Phase 4. I visit the site at that time or later.
Phase 5. Depositions are taken of parties involved.
Phase 6. I write a report. Depending upon which state the case is in, I may or may not be asked to write a report.
Phase 7. The experts' depositions are taken; ideally the plaintiff's expert is deposed before the defense expert.
Phase 8. There is usually a mediation or settlement conference, which the expert typically does not attend.
Phase 9. Trial or settlement, which may be followed by an appeal, extending the case for several years and can result in a re-trial.

Doing the Depositions

My experience has been that the lawyers for both sides come to where I am if I am living in a place they want to visit, i.e., San Diego, or Seattle. Otherwise, I go to them. More recently, I work with them by videoconference, or by Skype with a Court Reporter, so no one has to travel. In the interest of time and expense, I prefer the latter. Also, with the advances in technology, along with Google photos, and other photos, I may not visit the site until it goes to trial, so there is no need to go to that location, in advance of trial.

The length of time of the deposition also varies by state. I have had depositions that have gone into a second day; I had one deposition that was eleven hours long. Some states limit them to two hours. Sometimes the depositions are contentious. The opposing lawyers nearly came to blows in one of my depositions. And there were only three of us in the room. I was scoping out means of escape. In another, I insisted upon leaving a Miami deposition because my car was in a parking garage, and it was getting dark. I walked out, and the opposing attorney said, as I was leaving: "Let the record show that the expert is leaving the deposition." I replied: "Let the record show that I am leaving for reasons of security". The expert on the other side, got up, and without his lawyer's permission, escorted me to my car. He was an ex-police officer with the Miami Police Department and a gentleman, proving that chivalry is not dead in Miami.

Expert witness trial testimony may be preceded by Daubert Testimony, written or verbal, in which you must qualify under the Daubert rules, written about in my *Social Science and the Law* dissertation and the subsequent book.[23] It is well-defined on several legal sites, with references, on line.[24] Briefly, it is explained below:[25]

THE DAUBERT STANDARD
The *Daubert* standard provides a rule of evidence regarding the admissibility of expert witnesses' testimony in federal court. The *Daubert* standard came about from the U.S. Supreme Court case, *Daubert v. Merrell Dow Pharmaceuticals, 509 U.S. 579 (1993)*. *Daubert* is a guideline for expert admissibility for federal cases, but many states also adopted the *Daubert*. An Expert's Testimony or expert's report can be challenged and excluded if it does not meet the *Daubert* standard.
The Federal Rules of Evidence 702 states that a witness who is qualified as an expert by knowledge, skill, experience, training, or education may testify in the form of an opinion or otherwise if:
(a) the expert's scientific, technical, or other specialized knowledge will help the trier of fact to understand the evidence or to determine a fact in issue;
(b) the testimony is based on sufficient facts or data;
(c) the testimony is the product of reliable principles and methods; and
(d) the expert has reliably applied the principles and methods to the facts of the case.
Federal court cases and more than half of the states use *Daubert*. [End Daubert Definition].

Visiting the Crime Sites

When I am mentoring or giving speeches, one of the most frequent questions asked by young girls or women is: "What do you wear to a crime site?" Since my work is long after the crime has been committed, it's nothing like when a police officer, detective, forensic scientist, or coroner goes to the crime site. It may be years later. "What's important, girls, is that you **not** wear high heels". You may be crawling under stairwells, walking through fields, along riverbanks, in the woods, across hot parking lots, deserted parking structures, and in all kinds of weather, especially pounding rain, like at a site in Las Vegas, where it never rains.

Often, the lawyer wants you to visit the site at the time of day the crime was committed. Since 75 percent of crimes occur at night, you are, therefore, frequently visiting the crime site at night. One night, I was sitting with an attorney in his car by a convenience store at midnight, on the border of Ohio and Kentucky. It was a case where a fight had occurred, all caught on camera, and the perpetrator had said: "F--- this sh--. I'm 'gonna' kill someone". As the attorney and I were replaying the incident, I turned to him and said: "Why are we here? We've seen the place, so we can discuss this somewhere else." He did not have to be asked twice.

For a visit to a San Francisco crime site, the crime had occurred at 10:30 pm. My lawyer wanted me to see the site, but he lived in the suburbs and did not want to come back to the city at the time, so he said I could just, "hail a cab". Fortunately, my super-sleuth girlfriend from Dallas was in San Francisco with me, and she and I hailed a cab and went to the crime site together to the dark, isolated corner on Market Street. Obviously, we had the cab driver wait for us, so we were all in danger at this deserted outdoor ATM. Our Sikh cab driver, followed us around, and kept mumbling, mostly to himself: "Why would your lawyer make you girls do this?" I guess because chivalry *is* dead in San Francisco.

In Las Vegas, Arnie and I wanted to see where the murderer of this crime lived, and the attorney said he could not take us there because the neighborhood was too dangerous. This, coming from an attorney who was driving a bullet-proof Mercedes, custom-made in Germany, and "packing heat". We didn't insist.

At another site in Las Vegas, the attorney insisted we go to a fast food drive-through, where there had been a gang shoot-out and that we go inside the restaurant—not him, of course, just us. Arnie and I went in and actually saw drug transactions taking place with the employees. Needless to say, my words to Arnie were, "Let's get out of here'. For another one of *this same lawyer's cases*, he drove us to a "really bad area" in his big, black Escalade, to a motel that had a drug dealer on the corner of each balcony, with visible guns. He wanted us (not him) to walk around. That is not to happen", I said, "I get the idea. Let's get out of here". In fact, that is the most frequent thing I say when I visit a crime site—"Let's get out of here'.

At one of our Miami site visits, an off-duty, bulky police officer accompanied us for protection, who had been hired by the attorney. Unfortunately, the Cuban female attorney was wearing stilettos and a short, sleeveless, tight sheath dress (That's Miami). We did not need the attention that she drew in this particular housing project. The African-American off-duty officer stood in the center of the courtyard and watched, somehow in four directions, as we did our inspection of apartment 301. As residents started to gather, inside and outside of the gated courtyard, the police officer was the one that hollered up to us: "Let's get out of here".

Testifying at Trial

There are a lot of phases, discussed above, before you reach trial and nine times out of ten, I never end up testifying at trial. The case settles, or it is is dismissed, before that. When I do testify, it is usually for a couple of hours on the stand, but it has gone to four or more, in rare situations. Before taking up my individual cases in the next chapters, a couple of personal experiences are shared below, which are all part of "the experience" of being a forensic sociologist and expert witness. These kinds of days leave me wondering: "Why", or "Why me"?

A Bad Day in Detroit

This day in Detroit nearly ended my consulting career, and I concentrated more on expert witnessing after this experience. It was snowing on this February, 2007, morning, when I left Sioux Falls, and it was snowing when I reached Detroit. Luckily, I was warmly attired in fur-lined black leather tall boots and a heavy tan trench coat, with layers of clothes underneath.. At the airport, I grabbed my luggage and went outside and hailed a taxi. The driver loaded my newly-purchased black Brighton luggage into the back of his van, and I settled into the back seat on the right passenger side. Five minutes into our trip, the back window exploded and blew out, covering me with glass shards. The Middle-Eastern taxi driver turned around and said: "Who would be shooting at us?"

I said "I don't know, I just got here" and hit the floor with my cell phone in hand. Then, the driver went on to say, "Shall we pull over?" I said "No. That would be the worst thing you could do, if someone is shooting at us". "Just drive to the nearest service station" (which I know is probably the next least safe place to be). While on the floorboard of the car, I immediately phoned Arnie and said: "I am in a cab in Detroit, and the back window has just been blown out." His reply, I kid you not, was: "Is your new Brighton luggage okay"? I said "No, it's covered with glass shards, as am I". More sympathetic now, and apparently realizing the seriousness of the matter, he said: "Honey, I am sorry. Hang up, call 911, and keep me posted." I hung up and dialed 911.

The taxi driver and I arrived at a service station within minutes, and the police officers arrived almost immediately thereafter. In the meantime, there were no more shots, and the driver had called his company to report the incident. Another taxi from his company arrived simultaneously to take me to my destination, while I left the driver and the police, with my business card, to figure out what had happened, and I would not be late for my meeting. When I told my client, they were surprised and shocked at my story and apologized for Detroit. That was probably not the first time they had apologized for Detroit. I never heard back from the police, or the cab driver, so I don't know if they were gun shots or if the back window imploded on itself, which that type of car (which shall remain unnamed) had experienced.

My client in Detroit was one of the *Dollar-type stores*, which I will refer to fictionally as *Whole Dollar*. I was hired, as I am with my other clients, to analyze their crime vulnerability, in the area surrounding their stores, and at the stores, and then prepare a robbery and violence prevention plan and report for appropriate security measures. When deciding where I should visit to make site assessments, the client had picked Detroit. When they called to tell me that, I said: "I would rather not go to Detroit in February". The Corporate Security Manager, said: "They picked Detroit specifically because they want you to see the worst stores in the worst neighborhoods in the country." Translated, this means the highest crime stores in the highest crime neighborhoods, and originally I was just concerned about the weather in Detroit.

Upon my arrival in the replacement cab, we transferred to their corporate van, and six of us (at least) started our tour of visiting thirteen sites in one day. It would go like this: "Out of the van, walk to the store, stomp snow off boots, and enter store, remove coat, shake snow off coat, meet the clerks on duty, meet with the managers, tour the store, see the back of the store, and get back into the van and debriefed about what we had seen and learned" . . . thirteen times, we did this. It didn't happen on this trip, but often when I go into a convenience store for a site visit, wearing my tan trench coat, and accompanied by a burly security manager, also in a tan trench coat, the kids shopping (or shoplifting) in the back will yell: "FBI" and run out of the store. Kids. What are you going to do? This is the same security manager, by the way, who would say about his convenience stores: "You've seen one store, you've seen them all". I was about ready to tell *Whole Dollar* the same thing about their stores.

On this day, however, the client got their wish because I saw and heard about things I have never seen or heard about before. At one store, they told me that when the security camera company employee was installing the surveillance cameras, by the cash register, two masked armed robbers held them up, before the camera was operable, so they never got a picture of the robbers. The group would show me new stores where the air conditioner/heating units had been installed the night before and stolen overnight. They would show me city block after city block of real estate with stores and buildings that have been abandoned since the riots in 1967.

I was in Detroit, in 1968, attending the University of Michigan in Ann Arbor for a summer school program on advanced survey research methods for my Master's Degree in Sociology, but none of us in the program ever went into downtown Detroit. I landed at the airport in the summer of 1968 and went directly to the campus in Ann Arbor, so I had not seen the damages from the riots at the time. The group in the *Whole Dollar* corporate van explained that none of this business area, through which we were driving, had been rebuilt. A trend at this time was for copper companies to hire homeless men to climb up in the high floors of the buildings late at night and steal the copper for re-sale. "Where is OSHA when you need them?"

As we drove down the street in an especially rough residential neighborhood, I asked the corporate group: "Why are there teddy bears hanging in the trees?" There was a long pause before one of the security managers put forth the answer: "Each teddy bear represents a child that has been murdered here." I said" "I am so sorry", and we all rode in silence for a few minutes, as we continued our drive to yet another store and yet another story.

My client was, at this period of time, going in and buying up stores in Detroit, on the cheap, which had been vacated by a large drug store chain. That chain was literally "getting out of the neighborhoods" because of the high crime. I pointed out to the group that there was a reason for that, and that the other drugstore chain had also been one of my clients. At the locations, I always make a point of talking individually to security guards and clerks. In the past, I had talked to the security guard posted at this same drugstore chain, in Washington, D. C., and he said: "It is humiliating to be a security guard here because they steal things right in front of our eyes, and they know we aren't allowed to stop them or physically touch them. By the time we call the police, they are long gone." Then he added, while shaking his head: "The worst part is when groups of young women, mothers probably, come in with their own paper and plastic bags and fill them up with Pampers and then run out, and I am helpless to do anything." I never give feedback in these interviews. I just gave him a look of sympathy and thanked him for his time; but his story and dilemma became part of my proposed plan for the drugstore chain.

A Bad Day at the Miami Airport

On one of my expert witness trips, I nearly quit expert witnessing. It was Wednesday morning, July 21, 2011, when Arnie and I set out to fly from Miami, where we lived, to New York City for four days for a trial, where I would testify. In NYC, we were to take a cab to the Hilton Millennium and meet with lawyers at 6 PM that day. I was to testify in Federal Court the next day on Friday, the 22nd, in a case of a multi-million pharmaceutical cargo heist and theft from a truck stop in Antioch, Tennessee, which had been carried out by an organized Cuban gang out of Miami. Usually, I only do violent crime cases, but I have also done the civil cases on some multi-million dollar pharmaceutical and jewelry heists.

Arnie's and my plane was scheduled to leave at 12:14pm and arrive in NYC at 3:25. As always, we arrived the appointed two hours ahead of schedule at the airport, allowing time to eat lunch before our flight. Delta flies from Concourse H, which is where we first ate our lunch and then boarded the plane on schedule from Gate H-14 for our 12:14 flight. We settled in comfortably, and I started working on my case, and Arnie started reading a book. A few minutes later, the Captain said we all had to disembark and take everything with us because there was a valve leak and they would be jacking up the plane, and it may or may not leave in an hour.

We were then told unless we had international connections, we couldn't even stand in line to find another flight. We had to just go somewhere else or call the Delta hot-line. We went to Gate H-11 because they had a 2:36pm flight from Miami to NYC-Kennedy airport. By the time we got to the head of the line, that flight was booked, and we were put on standby. We waited there until they boarded, and we did not make the cut, so we proceeded to H-17 to wait for the 4:06pm flight from Miami to NYC. On that one, we were the first two standbys, and up until the last minute, it looked like two confirmed passengers were not going to arrive within the final ten minute deadline, and we were at the head of the line to take their place. However, one of the two arrived, and so a single passenger only was allowed to take our place. Since we were flying together, we did not make the flight.

By then it was 4pm, and we were finally confirmed, *not on standby*, on the 7pm. "Ah, three more hours to kill, and that's not all, by then Delta had given us each coupons!" We found a very nice restaurant next to the International Concourse J and ate our way through the menu, spending twice what the coupons were worth and watching a full-blown afternoon Miami thunderstorm with rain from our window seat at the restaurant.

We returned to Gate H-05 for our 7pm flight, and I took out my black leather Coach brief case with the legal case in it and continued to work, noting that a lot of our 12:14pm plane partners were also waiting for this flight. None of us were smiling. We were to board at 6:30pm, so at 6:20pm, I contacted my lawyer in NYC by email and said "If there are any changes, let me know by 6:30, before we board". I immediately received a return message that said "DO NOT BOARD YOUR PLANE. CALL ME". I called him, and the senior partner of the firm excitedly said: "You do not have to come to New York to testify after all. We won. You have done your job by just being on call at the airport, and you do not even have to travel or testify. Just go home and have a glass of wine". He added: "The last thing the Federal judge said that day was: "Shucks, I was looking forward to meeting Dr. Erickson." Little things like that can make my day.

Good news and good advice about going home and drinking wine, but we had to locate our luggage that had been rebooked at least four times that day. It took another hour to find out that our luggage was in fact in New York, without us, and they hoped to get it back sometime that night (or week). So, after nine hours in the Miami airport, we grabbed a cab. In the cab, we looked at each other, shell-shocked and confused, and I said to Arnie: "Now, what do we do with the next four days and the rest of our lives?" At home, I had that glass of wine, recommended by my attorney, and Arnie mused that it had altogether been a lovely day with my uninterrupted attention, for a change, good food, and his favorite thing to do, which is people watching. I reflected on the fact that all day, a public announcement was being made saying what time it was, and I had also been noticing the signs all over the airport saying "Miami International Airport (MIA)". And I thought how apt--Missing in Action--which applied to us, our original cancelled plane, our three other missed planes, and our luggage. We did not receive our luggage that night as promised. It arrived a few days later, but we were so glad to be home, and not having to go to trial in New York, that we did not care. Any time I don't have to testify, I am happy.

The four individual cases, which I have selected to include in this book were each perpetrated by serial killers. My involvement starts, with the *aftermath*, which is after the violent crime, when the location is sued, and then I am called to serve either as an expert witness for the defense or plaintiff.

Stephen Hawking's recent quote underscores the point of the evil of the perpetrators, in these particular cases, in the next four chapters, when he recently warned: "Aggression threatens to destroy us all."[26] He said this during a tour of London's Science Museum and called for greater empathy. In the cases, you will read about here, the perpetrators are aggressive; they have no empathy; and they personify true evil.

CHAPTER SEVEN: WORKING THE CASES

CHAPTER EIGHT

~

METH MURDERS – GARCIA VS. ALLSUP'S

Elizabeth Garcia, a 26-year-old, Hispanic female, mother of three, and a college student, was working as a cashier alone at night at an Allsup's convenience store in Hobbs, NM, on January 15, 2002. It was her second night on the job of the 11pm to 7am shift. At 2:30am, a tragedy would occur that would end her life. A timeline, taken from the police investigation indicates the sequence of events beginning at 1:30am.

Time Line of Elizabeth Garcia's Murder
1:30am – Elizabeth was on the phone with her cousin. 1:30am –A guard from the local college, arrived. The receipt says his sale was at 1:40, but it was 1:30 because it the clock was set 10 minutes fast. Elizabeth set the phone down, while the guard is there, and then she and her cousin continue talking after he leaves. 2:00am – Elizabeth tells her cousin that a customer is pulling in, and she has to hang up and will call back in 15 minutes, but she never calls back. 2:14am – There is a "No sale" receipt. It says 2:24 but was set 10 minutes fast. 2:41am – A friend of Elizabeth's arrives at store and finds that Elizabeth is not there, and he calls Elizabeth's brother to tell him.

When the police arrived, after being notified by Elizabeth's brother, they found that Elizabeth's vehicle was still parked in front of the store, unlocked. Elizabeth's brother told them she usually left her car unlocked and the keys under the driver's seat. The detective could not locate the keys and observed nothing out of place and nothing showed there was a struggle in the store. The cash register was open, and the cash drawer was on the counter. The north cash register was opened by the store manager, when she arrived, and she discovered that all of the money had been removed, which turned out to be only twelve dollars missing, [an indication that this was never about robbery]. The manager said that it appeared that Elizabeth had made all of her "money drops" and the other chores that were required. There were no prints. The counter top had been cleaned, and there were no smudges. It appeared, law enforcement reported, that Garcia had just "walked out of the business".

The panic alarm, which was to be worn by clerks, was not located, and so it had not set off the alarm, when Elizabeth left the store. The alarm would have alerted authorities that she had left the store. The detective was told by Elizabeth's brother that Elizabeth's son had the alarm in his backpack at school.

It was not until 2pm the next afternoon on 1/16/04, that two men discovered Elizabeth Garcia's body. They called from the Allsup's on Sanger and Jefferson to advise they had located a body off the road on West Sanger. Garcia's body was found in a vacant field near a dirt road, just 11 minutes from the store where she had been working. Her killer had stabbed her fifty-six times and slit her throat. He stabbed her chest, abdomen, back, and hip, and she had other injuries on her hands and arms. He stabbed her with such force that it broke her bones.

Garcia was clothed when she was stabbed and when she was found. Police found tire tracks and footprints at the scene. The blood and scrapes on the ground indicated that Garcia had been dragged from the passenger side of a car. The discovery of her body led to one of the most complicated criminal investigations, with more possible suspects, than I have seen in any other case.

Figure 14 portrays a diagram of the victim's relationships among the other individuals involved and at least eight possible suspects. The information comes from the public information from the media and the combined criminal trial appeal.[27] Names are changed throughout, except for the victim, the murderer, and his other murder victim.

The photos of victim Elizabeth Garcia and perpetrator Paul Lovett are shown below.

The Victim – Elizabeth Garcia

Her Killer-Paul Lovett

Figure 14: Garcia Murder Suspect Diagram

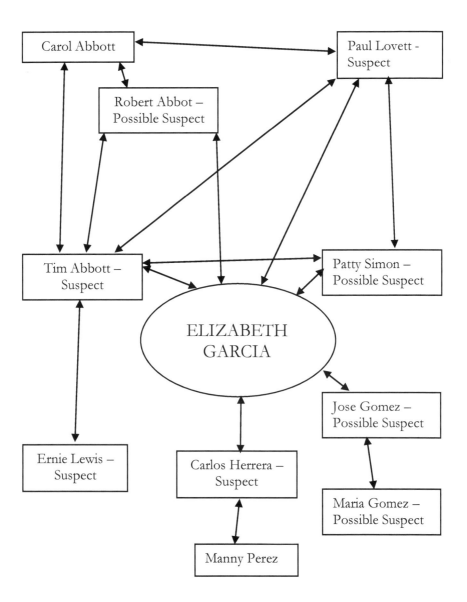

As shown in Figure 14, these were the key people and possible suspects, with relevant information, discussed below, and the people who were investigated by the Hobbs Police Department.

PERSONS OF INTEREST OR WITH INFORMATION

Elizabeth Garcia – Victim on night shift at Allsup's at about 2:30 AM on 1/16/02. H/F/26, mother of three, estranged from her husband, Carlos Herrera, her second night at this store. DNA from more than two individuals was found on Garcia's panties. Tim Abbott, Ernie Lewis, and Jose Gomez were eliminated from DNA.

Jose Gomez – He was having an affair with Elizabeth. He went to the store and found her missing and called her brother. Jose Gomez was married to Maria Gomez and had another girlfriend, whom he called on the way to the store that night. **Suspect.**

Maria Gomez – Knew her husband, Jose Gomez, was having an affair with Elizabeth, and she had made threatening phone calls to Elizabeth the week before and called her house the night of the murder. She told police she hated Elizabeth and" didn't care that she was dead".

Pedro Lopez. Maria Gomez told the police that in addition to her husband, Garcia may also have been dating Pedro Lopez, who works at a body shop. **Suspect.**

Robert Abbott – Tim Abbot's father--Paul Lovett's father-in-law--worked at an auto store with Elizabeth, and was admittedly infatuated with her. He had offered her a job in his home, and pointed out Elizabeth to Paul Lovett at some point. Robert Abbott had bought Elizabeth gifts and written her notes, but she told him to stop, and he had a few months earlier. **Suspect.**

Tim Abbott – Robert's Abbott's son—Paul Lovett's brother-in-law--knew of his father's infatuation with Elizabeth and by his and other's accounts, he did not like it. Jim claimed he did *not* have sex with Garcia. Jim knew that his dad offered her a job and thought she was going to take it and claims he did not know she was going to work for Allsup's. He told several people that he killed Elizabeth Garcia,

---

and he was seen with scratches and blood on his clothes that early morning. DNA tests were negative on him for Garcia. The night of Garcia's murder, Tim Abbott hid the white Mustang of a friend's that he had borrowed in Carol Abbott and Paul Lovett's garage. He shaved his head and eyebrows that night and Paul shaved his head and eyebrows also on the night of the 15th. A friend said that between 3 and 5 on the 16th, Tim Abbott told him that he had killed Garcia. He had scratches on his hands and blood on his pants and he said he killed the "Allsup's' bitch, and she won't be fucking my dad anymore." **Suspect.**

Carol Abbott Lovett– Tim abbot's sister—Robert's daughter, and Paul's wife--at the time of the Garcia murder. Jim parked his white mustang in her and Paul's garage the night of the Garcia murder.

Francis Abbott – Later married to Paul Lovett, after the Garcia murder, and at the time of the Patty Simon murder in 2003. She turned over a knife from a hamper--a possible weapon.

Ernie Lewis – was with Tim Abbott the night of Garcia's murder until sunrise, along with another friend. **Suspect.**

Carlos Herrera – Elizabeth's husband (or common-law husband) and father of her three children, separated for three years. At midnight on the 16th, he came to the police station to tell them that he did not do it. He said he was the father of the three children with Elizabeth, but they do not live together. [While there, the police arrested him on an outstanding deported felon hit]. While he was in jail, he called Manny Perez and told him to get rid of his (Carlos') cell phone and clothes. There was a restraining order against Carlos: *Prohibiting Domestic Violence against Carlos Herrera*, taken out by Elizabeth Garcia on 9/12/00. **Suspect.**

Manny Perez – Carlos' crew boss. On a recorded police call, from jail, Carlos asked him to get rid of his clothes and cell phone. Perez at first denied knowledge of this but subsequently turned over the cell phone to the police. Perez was killed in an oil field accident in October 2002.

Patty Simon – Patty Simon said she was in Odessa with her boyfriend that night and traveled to Hobbs for court on 1/16/02. She talked with Tim Abbott during the day of 1/16/02. Then, she was subsequently murdered on May 14, 2003. A friend of Paul Lovett, they used meth together, including the night of her murder. She also talked to him multiple times the night of Garcia's murder. Two sources said she was involved with the Garcia murder. Mother of 4. **Suspect and Victim.**

Paul Lovett – Suspect W/M/22. He was Robert Abbott' son-in law, Carol Abbott's husband, and Tim Abbott's brother in law. Robert had pointed Elizabeth out to Paul and told Paul he (Robert) was infatuated with her. Steven parked a white mustang in Carol's and Paul's garage the night of the murder. Paul and Tim Abbott shaved their heads and eyebrows that night. Paul was friends with and did meth with Patty Simon, including the night he murdered Patty. After Patty Simon's death, Paul said his DNA would probably be found on Garcia, so he became a **Prime Suspect**. He was ultimately convicted of the murders of both Elizabeth Garcia and Patty Simon.

The initial police investigation was full of lies and misleading information from people of interest—more than I see in most cases. Many of the people involved admitted to or were known to use meth. Some of the information, extracted above, indicates that Tim Abbott was the prime suspect, in large part because he said on 12/17/03 that he had killed Elizabeth. [No explanation was ever advanced for why he confessed to a murder he did not commit].

It was not until the second murder--that of Patty Simon--that the two murders were both connected to one person—Paul Lovett. Here is the description of the Patty Simon murder.[28]

Approximately sixteen months later, on May 14, 2003, workers found another young woman, Patty Simon, dead in a caliche pit on the outskirts of Hobbs. Deceased, with a shirt pulled over her head and blunt trauma to the forehead and cut along the throat area. On the same day, a delivery man found Lovett lying on the side of a road outside of Hobbs, shirtless. This gentleman said he was the person that had shown Paul the pit in 2000 where Patty's body was found.

Another female friend had traveled to Axis, AL with Paul Lovett the latter part of January 2002 in a 1996 tan Ford Taurus GL. The police brought it back in June 2003. In June 2003, Lovett was interviewed and said that Tim Abbott had asked Lovett to provide semen and pubic hairs in a condom, so his

DNA might be located on Elizabeth Garcia's body. On June 25, 2002, Lovett's pubic area had been shaven, so no pubic hair could be collected, but his blood and hair samples matched the DNA collected from Garcia's panties. According to a friend of Lovett's, Paul Lovett was hurt in an oilfield accident in September of 2001 and couldn't work after that. Paul Lovett was charged with the kidnapping and murder of Elizabeth Garcia. He said he didn't kill Patty, but he didn't deny that he had killed Garcia. Incriminating information is shown below, taken from the Lovett appeal following his trial in 2007 for the combined Garcia and Simon murders[29]

From Lovett Appeal

In addition to testimony about where [Patty] Simon was found and Defendant's (Lovett's) predicament that morning—claiming to have been with Simon the night before, the State introduced testimony and photographic evidence documenting the fact that Simon was also brutally murdered. For example, the State introduced testimony and photographs documenting that Simon suffered severe, blunt-force trauma to her head and neck. She had a broken nose and radiating skull fractures. One of her eyes was ruptured, and there were numerous lacerations, bruises, and other injuries to her arms, hands, and the rest of her body, consistent with "defensive wounds." There was a "large, gaping, incised wound or slash across the upper part of her throat" and obvious injuries to her legs and genitalia. Either the cut to her throat or the blunt-force injuries caused Simon's death.

Unlike Garcia, police found Simon nude from her bra line down. Her shirt was pulled up over her head. Her legs were spread, and her underwear was around her ankles. Simon's injuries were consistent with, but not necessarily conclusive of, a sexual penetration. No semen was found at the scene.

Simon's car was parked at the scene, with a lot of blood found in and around it, including in the trunk. A cigarette butt was found sitting in the opening to the gas tank, and police collected cigarette butts found on the ground in the area. Only one type of footprint was found near Simon's body.

Much of the physical evidence tied Defendant to the Simon murder. Investigators found Defendant's shirt, which was bloody, under a pile of rocks near Simon's body. DNA on cigarette butts found all around the Simon scene matched Defendant's DNA. Simon's blood was on Defendant's shoes and underwear. The numerous shoe prints around Simon's body were consistent with the shoes Defendant wore that day. A fiber found on Simon's hand was consistent with jeans, and Defendant was wearing jeans the day Simon was killed. Defendant's underwear had DNA on it that could not exclude Simon, but could not conclusively be identified as her DNA. DNA found on Defendant's penis matched Simon with a high likelihood; the likelihood that someone else would match the DNA collected from his penile swab was 1 in 410 to 1 in 670. [End Appeal Information]

In the 2012 decision, the court reversed Defendant's conviction for first-degree murder in relation to Garcia and upheld his conviction for first-degree murder and criminal sexual penetration in relation to Simon. Lovett was subsequently retried for the Garcia case and was found guilty again in 2014 of first degree murder of Elizabeth Garcia. There was never a conclusion as to how she was taken from the store, or why Paul Lovett murdered her or Simon.

The likely underlying reason for the murder of Garcia and Simon is Lovett's use of meth, which multiple friends, relatives, and acquaintances testified about. He had been up for days, reportedly, at the time of Garcia's murder. A Department of Justice study, discussed in the paragraphs below, disclosed the fact that it was an epidemic in New Mexico at that time, and reported upon the relationship between the use of meth and violence.[30]

The New Mexico Meth Epidemic

Methamphetamine is an increasing drug threat to New Mexico. Throughout the state the availability and abuse of the drug are increasing. While most of the methamphetamine available in the state is smuggled across the border from Mexico, New Mexico law enforcement officials report an increase in the production and availability of locally produced methamphetamine. Mexican DTOs and Mexican criminal groups are the primary transporters and wholesale distributors of Mexico-produced methamphetamine in New Mexico;

Mexican criminal groups, OMGs, and local independent dealers control the production and wholesale distribution of locally produced methamphetamine. OMGs, prison and street gangs, and local independent dealers are the primary distributors of both Mexico- and locally produced methamphetamine at the retail level. The low cost and long-lasting euphoric effects of methamphetamine have attracted new users to the drug.

Psychological paranoia associated with methamphetamine may lead to homicidal and suicidal tendencies. Abusers of methamphetamine frequently commit crimes and violent acts to obtain money to support their drug habits or as a result of the "tweaking" stage of abuse. During the tweaking stage, the methamphetamine abuser often has not slept for days and, consequently, is extremely irritable. The "tweaker" also craves more methamphetamine, which results in frustration and contributes to anxiety and restlessness. In this stage, the abuser may become violent without provocation. [End Department of Justice Report].

Allsup's was sued in a civil premises liability suit, claiming foreseeability and lack of security. I served as one of at least three defense witnesses. I learned more about Hobbs, New Mexico and meth than I wanted to know in this case. Early on in the civil case, Arnie and I visited Hobbs, met with our lawyers, and then had lunch, alone together, without our lawyer. In a town this size, with under 30,000 population, when we went into the cafe, everyone looked up. People in booths turned to look, and people at the lunch counter swiveled their bar stools to see who was coming into the cafe.

In a small town, they do this for the most part to see if it is someone they know. If they do not know them, then they have to try to figure out who you are, which is typically done this way. The waitress comes up, pad and pencil in hand, and says: "What brings you to these parts?" We know *not* to say "We are working on a case", but rather, "Just traveling through". When we went to the crime site, we also reluctantly learned what caliche is. It's a type of road covering made up of a number of materials, including cement, and it fits with the complete barrenness of the desert. It was a lonely road by a lonely caliche pit, when Arnie and I pulled up in our rental car. There was not a pickup or a person in sight in the middle of a hot day, as we stepped out of the car. It was completely silent, except for the sound of the oil rigs pumping up and down, up and down, and up and down. Arnie and I walked a little ways and looked around, and then we looked at each other, and I, predictably, said, "Let's get out of here".

One of the considerations by the defense was that Lovett was an irrational actor, psychopath, and on meth. A review of the table below demonstrates these factors. I have checked the items that I believe apply to Lovett, based on the evidence from the criminal case and trial. The defense argument in the civil case was that it is difficult, if not impossible, to defend against an "irrational actor", whether they are irrational by nature of psychopathy or drug or alcohol use.

Paul Lovett Psychopathy Check List

√ GLIB and SUPERFICIAL CHARM

√ GRANDIOSE SELF-WORTH

√ NEED FOR STIMULATION or PRONENESS TO BOREDOM

√ PATHOLOGICAL LYING

√ CONNING AND MANIPULATIVENESS

√ LACK OF REMORSE OR GUILT

√ SHALLOW AFFECT

√ CALLOUSNESS and LACK OF EMPATHY

√ PARASITIC LIFESTYLE

√ POOR BEHAVIORAL CONTROLS

√ PROMISCUOUS SEXUAL BEHAVIOR

EARLY BEHAVIOR PROBLEMS

√ LACK OF REALISTIC, LONG-TERM GOALS

√ IMPULSIVITY

√ IRRESPONSIBILITY

√FAILURE TO ACCEPT RESPONSIBILITY FOR OWN ACTIONS

√ MANY SHORT-TERM MARITAL RELATIONSHIPS

JUVENILE DELINQUENCY

REVOCATION OF CONDITION RELEASE

CRIMINAL VERSATILITY

√ = The item applies to Paul Lovett. No check mark indicates it does not apply or information was not available to make an informed decision.

In the analysis above, the indication is that Paul Lovett was a psychopath, according to a majority of the factors. For some of the factors, there is no information available. We know he was high on meth at the time of one or both of the murders; thus, making him an irrational actor at the time of both murders.

The civil case of Garcia vs. Allsup's went to trial, but I was not called to testify at the civil trial. One of the defense experts, who testified, opined on the role of Lovett's meth use; and that the crime was not foreseeable; and that the store had met the standards of the industry at the time. The suit was settled shortly before a jury reported their verdict against Allsup's. The terms of the settlement were not disclosed.[31]

CHAPTER NINE

~

TIME TO SAY GOODNIGHT - MASENGILL VS. SHELL

A beautiful young woman, 19/W/F, was filling her car with gas at a Shell station in St. Louis MO right across the highway from an airport hotel.. It was Sunday, October 25th, 1992, at 4:30 pm, so it was still daylight. She went into the station and paid ten dollars for her gas. Upon returning to her car, a man came up behind her, showed a gun, and forced her to climb from the driver's side to the passenger side of the car. He began driving and said: "Don't worry I'm not going to hurt you. I just need to borrow your car for a while. If you do what I say, I promise nothing is going to happen to you."[32]   Then, he drove her to an isolated wooded area.

Once at the location, he raped her, and then he walked her to the edge of a tree-line. He pointed a gun directly at her, and said, "It's time to say goodnight". She turned to run, as he shot her in the head. She fell down, and he turned around and returned to her car. From there, he drove her car back to the station. There, he went into the station and, showed the same gun, and robbed the clerk of $330.00. He walked back to his truck, got in, and drove out of the station.

In the meantime, Jamie Masengill, the teenager, who had been abducted from the station, raped, and shot, did not die. In the early morning hours of the next day, she regained consciousness and was found by a couple walking their dog. Jamie had survived one of the worst abductions, rapes, and shootings that St. Louis had seen. She was in a coma for three days after being found. During that time, the police had arrested her boyfriend for the murder, and it was only after she regained consciousness that she could tell them that he was not the one who did it.

Police later learned that the suspected killer might have been staying across the road at the an airport hotel. [The card reader that hotels often use for entry to each floor does not guarantee your safety on that floor. The person next door to you may be a rapist or murderer.]

With the new information that the police learned from Jamie about the description of the perpetrator and the abduction, the investigation was underway, but nothing led them to the sociopathic perpetrator at that time--nothing. Unknown to the authorities, this is what James Wood did over the next several months, before it was learned that this serial killer, serial rapist, and serial robber was her abductor. They only learned this, and pieced it together, after he killed again.

After James drove into the Missouri night, he stayed overnight on the interstate at a motel, and then left early the next morning, driving across Kansas and Colorado, stopping near Denver for the night. We know what happened next, and we know about the monster—James Wood—in part from the book *Eye of the Beast*, as described in the next paragraphs. [33]

That night, James Wood joined strangers for a drink, at the bar, and during their conversation, he left for a short while. He needed money, so he went to the pizza place by his motel and robbed them of $700.00; then, he returned to his table of newly-found friends. When the police arrived with sirens at the robbery site, James reportedly showed no sign of interest or involvement. He returned to his hotel, slept that night, and the next morning, he headed to Cheyenne, WY. From there, he went on to Pocatello, ID, where he had left more than twenty-five years before. He was going there because he knew he had relatives he could use there.

He hadn't even planned to go to St. Louis, on October 25, 1992. He was driving from Alton, IL to Pocatello and was agitated because he had raped his 14-year-old-stepdaughter, saying it was her fault because she was wearing skimpy clothing. He knew he had to get away from Louisiana and Illinois because he had not been released that long for a second time (earlier for robbery) from Angola State Penitentiary in Louisiana. He had served only six years of a ten year sentence and was released for good behavior. His crime had been slitting the throats of two teenage girls, and rape, but the charge was reduced to aggravated assault. A white male at 44 years of age, at this point, he had three children from three marriages.

In Pocatello, he looked up his cousin Dave Haggard, and he had been right about finding relatives he could use. During his time with him, he could never keep a job and did not pay rent. Haggard would find him jobs, feed him, and let him use his vehicle, later helped him get one of his own, with Haggard paying for it. The other cousins suspected that "Jimmy" may be trouble because of hearing of his "cutting up girls" in Louisiana and serving time for it. The cousins would eventually "bring him down", but in the meantime, James Wood lived with Haggard from the fall of 1992 until what would be his final crime perpetrated on June 29, 1993. Haggard would describe him as very neat and a nice guy, but he was committing crimes right in the city in which he lived.

This is the way his last murder, that of the 11-year-old newspaper girl, was described in court papers:[34]

State of Idaho vs. James Wood

Jeralee Underwood (Jeralee) resided in Pocatello, Idaho with her family. On June 29, 1993, James Wood (Wood) was visiting the home of a customer on Jeralee's paper route when she came by to make a collection. Wood followed Jeralee when she left, detained her with a false story, and forced her into his automobile. Wood held Jeralee captive for over a day, during which time he sexually molested her, then shot her in the head with a .22 caliber pistol and hid her body by covering it with brush. According to the findings of the district court: "Wood returned to the site of the murder, undressed the corpse, and mutilated the body by removing the sex organs and severing the arms, head, and legs. He threw the clothing and body parts into the Snake River. The body was later recovered, with the exception of the right hand and right calf."

Wood's cousin Haggard suspected the perpetrator was James because on the day of Jeralee's murder, James had washed his vehicle and vacuumed it. After he went back for his final acts with her, he took Haggard's pickup. When he returned, he similarly washed and vacuumed it. Haggard saved the contents of the vacuum bag and later went to the police and asked for assurance that they would arrest James at the same time they did a search warrant or he feared for his life.

Signs featuring Jeralee Underwood were posted at various locations across east Idaho. | EastIdahoNews.com. Photo above.[35]

James Edward Wood was charged with first degree murder and sentenced to death. | Idaho Department of Corrections. Photo below[36].

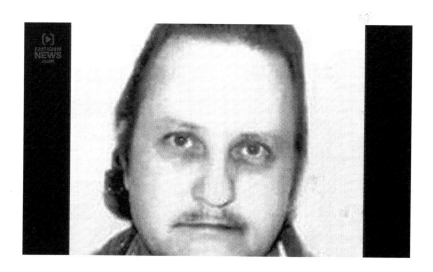

A summary chronicling the life of James Wood, from childhood, is given in the *Eye of the Beast* and provided below, with some fictionalization of names and places and bracketing added.

James Edward Wood
Information Researched and Summarized
by Jessica Weber, Heather Wells & John Wesley
Department of Psychology Radford University Radford, VA
24142-6946[37,38]

Date	Age	Life Event
12/09/1947	0	Born on December 9, 1947 as James Godwin.
1949	2	Father incarcerated at a federal prison. His mother, Hazel Godwin, took James and moved to Pocatello, Idaho and remarried shortly after.
1953	6	Developed a hatred for police/ authority figures
1955	8	Mother died in a potato processing plant fire.
1956	9	Started having violent sexual fantasies
1961	14	James received counseling at St. Anthony's Youth Correction Center in Idaho (one of 3 stays).
1961	14	Stole a car and set fire to dumpsters
1961	14	Became a ward of the state
1964	17	James was released from reform school under the condition that he leave the state and live with his natural father in Louisiana where he began to work in his father's business of selling and installing chain fences.
1964	17	He escaped from prison by threatening a guard's life with a knife (His only successful escape out of seven attempts)
1966	19	Killed a colt that was tied to a tree as a Christmas gift [for a neighbor's child].
1967	20	Married first wife, Angie Bell, and had a child. Angie filed for divorce a few months later after

		learning about James' sentence to prison.
1969	22	Wood commits his first rape
1974	27	Remarried Angie and had another child, but a few months later Angie filed for a final divorce.
1986	39	James was released from Angola State Penitentiary and moved to Texas and lived with his half-brother Earnest Arnold. Went to work as a truck driver for a carnival out of Tyler, Texas. Moved out of Arnold's home after Arnold disapproved of James' relationship with a gay man named Jimmy Twiggs that he had met at Angola.
1990	43	James injured his left hand, severely cutting three of his fingers. The fingers were surgically repaired but his hand still remained weak.
10/1992	45	Denver, Colorado – robbed a Pizza Hut.
10/31/1992	45	Pocatello, Idaho – James arrives at his cousin's, Dave Haggard, and asks for a place to live. Haggard agrees to let him stay until he could get back on his feet.
Fall 1992	45	Got a job as a dishwasher at Tina's Ox Bow Restaurant, but used his spare time to make paintings on old handsaws and began to sell them.
11/28/1992	45	Abducted and raped 15 year old Beth Edwards from a Pizza Hut parking lot.
1993	45	Robbed a Subway Sandwich Shop
Early Spring 1993	45	Wood raped a 14 year old Karen, Daughter of his girlfriend
1993	45	Robbed Sizzler Steak house in Salt Lake City
1993	45	Raped a Women after picking her up off street in Salt Lake City (same day as Sizzler Steak house Robbery)
06/29/1993	45	Wood abducted and killed Jeralee Underwood, age 10, a newspaper carrier in the area. He brought her into the woods and shot and dismembered her body as she got out to use the bathroom.
07/06/1993	45	Wood is arrested for the murder of Jeralee Underwood

01/14/1994	46	Wood is sentenced to death by lethal injection for the murder of Jeralee Underwood. Wood confessed to killing s Louisiana woman in 1976.
07/25/1994	47	Sixth district judge rejects Wood's appeal
10/09/1998	50	Idaho State Supreme Court rejects Wood's appeal for the third time
12/22/1998	51	Supreme Court justice O'Connor signed a stay of execution until Wood's death sentence appeal could be heard by the entire U.S Supreme Court
05/16/1999	51	U.S. Supreme Court refused to hear Wood's appeal
02/01/2004	56	Died from a heart attack while on death row.

General Information

Sex	Male
Race	White
Number of Victims	Convicted of killing 1(believed to have killed dozens), confessed to 2 murders, [may have been 30], raped 85 women, responsible for 185 robberies
Country where killing occurred	United States
States where killing occurred	LA, AR, ID
Cities where killing occurred	Pocatello, ID
Type of killer	Disorganized
Height	5'9" – 5'10"

Childhood Information

Date of birth	December 9, 1947
Location	Louisiana
Birth Order	Only child of mother (Hazel Godwin)

Number of siblings	One older step-brother (Earnest Arnold)
XYY?	Not determined
Raised by	Uncle and Aunt after mother died in 1955; due to James' problems the Wood relatives relinquished their custody and James became a ward of the state
Birth category	Youngest
Parent's marital status	Divorced; mother remarried
Family event	Father incarcerated at a federal prison when James was 2 years old; at this time James and his mother moved to Pocatello, ID where his mother remarried. His mother died in a fire while working in a potato factory when James was 8 years old. James was in school right across the street and watched the fire
Age of family event	2 & 8
Problems in school?	Yes
Teased while in school?	No
Physically attractive?	A 160-180lb Caucasian male with short brown hair – fit in and was not noticeable physically by others around him
Physical defect?	1990 – Severely injured 3 fingers on his left hand while using a power saw – had surgery, but still had problems using his hand.
Speech defect?	No

Head injury?	None reported
Physically abused?	James claimed he was physically abused by his step-father.
Psychologically abused?	James claimed he was psychologically abused by his step-father.
Sexually abused?	James claimed he was sexually abused by his step-father.
Father's occupation	Business selling and installing chain fences
Age of first sexual experience	9-years old had violent sexual fantasies
Age when first had intercourse	N/A
Mother's occupation	Worked in a potato factory
Father abused drugs/alcohol	N/A
Mother abused drugs/alcohol	None mentioned
Cognitive Ability	
Highest Grade in School	Most of teenage years he was in a youth correction center and attended a reform school in Idaho until 17.
Highest degree	Never received a diploma
Grades in school	[unknown]
IQ	N/A
Source of IQ information	N/A
Work History	
Served in the military?	No
Branch	N/A
Type of discharge	N/A
Saw combat duty	N/A

Killed enemy during service?	N/A
Applied for job as a cop?	No
Worked in law enforcement?	No
Fired from jobs?	James had trouble holding down jobs where he was fired or he just quit and would not return to that place of employment to work.
Types of jobs worked	Installed chain fences, carnival truck driver, painted old saws and metal milk jugs with wild life scenes for money & dishwasher, but he usually stole money to survive. Wood did not like to work because it was "too boring".
Employment status during series	Unemployed
Relationships	
Sexual preference	Heterosexual – homosexual tendencies began in prison
Marital status	Divorced
Number of children	3 – 2 sons and 1 daughter
Lives with his children	No
Living with	Cousin Dave Haggard
Triad	
Animal Torture	No [he shot a colt]
Fire setting	Yes
Bed wetting	No [I don't think this is known]
Killer Psychological Information	
Abused drugs?	N/A [I don't think this is known]

Abused alcohol?	Yes
Been to a psychologist?	No
Time in forensic hospital?	No
Diagnosis	Impulsive, anti-social, no conscience, lack of remorse, sexual sadism, violent outbursts, sensitive to criticism, unpredictable, loner [Unknown who gave this diagnosis]
Killer Criminal History	
Committed previous crimes?	Armed robbery and rape [and murder]
Spend time in jail?	Yes/incarcerated 3 times before murder conviction
Spend time in prison?	Served 4.5 years in Angola State Penitentiary (1967-1971). Served a second sentence of 6 years out of 10 for robbery and rape. He was released for good behavior.
Killed prior to series? Age?	?
Serial Killing	
Number of victims	Not certain – Convicted of 1 killing and suspected of multiple others [possibly 30]
Victim type	Young women
Killer age at start of series	29
Date of first kill in series	1975
Date of final kill in series	Summer of 1993
Gender of victims	Females
Race of victims	Caucasian
Age of victims	Early adolescent to teenager

Type of victim	Females/no particular preference
Method of killing	Shot in head; Jeralee Underwood was dismembered.
Weapon	Killer brought with him
Was gun used?	Yes
Type	Handgun (.22 semi-automatic)
Did killer have a partner?	No
Name of partner	N/A
Sex of partner	N/A
Type of serial killer	Disorganized lust
How close did killer live?	Lived within a few neighborhoods of the victims
Location of fist contact	Killer's home
Location of killing	Woods/near lake
Killing occurred in home of victim?	No
Killing occurred in home of killer?	No
Victim abducted or killed at contact?	Abducted
Behavior during Crimes	
Rape?	Yes
Tortured victims?	Yes
Stalked victims?	Jeralee - He knew her newspaper route
Overkill?	Jeralee – Killed and dismembered body
Quick & efficient?	Yes
Used blindfold?	No
Bound the victims?	No

After Death Behavior	
Sex with the body?	Yes
Mutilated body?	Yes
Ate part of the body?	No
Drank the victim's blood?	No
Posed the body	No
Took totem-body part	No
Took totem-personal item	No
Robbed victim or location	Yes
Disposal of Body	
Left at scene, no attempt to hide	No
Left at scene, hidden	Yes/Threw body into lake
Left at scene, buried	No
Moved, no attempt to hide	No
Moved, buried	Last killing
Cut-op and disposed of	Last killing
Moved, too home	No
Sentencing	
Date killer arrested	Tuesday, July 6, 1993
Date convicted	January 14, 1994
Sentence	Death
Killer executed?	No, but was on death row (died of natural causes)
Did killer plead NGRI [Not Guilty by Reason of Insanity]?	No

Was the NGRI plea successful?	N/A
Name and state of prison	Idaho State Penitentiary
Killer committed suicide?	No
Killer killed in prison?	No, died from a heart attack
Date of death	February 1, 2004

References
Adams, T., Brooks-Mueller, M., & Shaw, S. (1998). *Eye of the beast: The true story of serial killer James Wood*. Omaha, NE: Addicus Books, Inc.

39

[End of Radford University Analysis. Brackets throughout are mine].

As noted above, James Wood died in prison from a heart attack on February 1, 2005. He was 57 years old. Thus ended the life of a serial killer, serial rapist, and serial murderer. It is rare that someone would be all three because criminals are more likely to be one or the other. Further, the numbers are astounding that he may have committed as many as 30 murders, 85 rapes, and 180 robberies.

Civil Suit

The victim, Jamie Masengill, filed a civil suit against Shell Oil Station for her abduction, rape and assault. The complaint said that Shell was negligent, because they had no security personnel, no security system, the CCTV not functioning, the employees were not properly trained, and there were previous criminal incidents at the location, which would make the event foreseeable. I was retained as a defense expert for Shell.

The attorney for the defense was a young, white female, and she I and together visited the crime scene, shortly after I began work on the case. We visited the service station from which she was abducted and then drove out to the river where she had been raped, shot, and left for dead. The attorney and I spent some time looking around, imagining how it had transpired, and discussing the case. Then at the same time, we both apparently noticed it was getting dark because we looked at each other, and said simultaneously, "Let's get out of here". We rapidly walked back to her car, took off quickly, and never went back.

My opinion was that there was foreseeability of a crime, in that there had been prior criminal incidents at the station, but clearly nothing like this, and certain security measures were in place. The event occurred in 1992, so the historical context was critical in understanding what was expected at that time. The opinion I held was that there were security measures at the station, but you cannot protect against a sociopathic serial robber, serial murderer, and serial rapist, who has no fear of being caught. Below, I analyze his psychopathy, based on the evidence in the criminal and civil cases.

James Wood Psychopathy Check List

√ GLIB and SUPERFICIAL CHARM

√ GRANDIOSE SELF-WORTH

√ NEED FOR STIMULATION or PRONENESS TO BOREDOM

√ PATHOLOGICAL LYING

√ CONNING AND MANIPULATIVENESS√

√ LACK OF REMORSE OR GUILT

√ SHALLOW

√ CALLOUSNESS and LACK OF EMPATHY

√ PARASITIC LIFESTYLE

√ POOR BEHAVIORAL CONTROLS

√ PROMISCUOUS SEXUAL BEHAVIOR

√ EARLY BEHAVIOR PROBLEMS

√ LACK OF REALISTIC, LONG-TERM GOALS

√ IMPULSIVITY

√ IRRESPONSIBILITY

√FAILURE TO ACCEPT RESPONSIBILITY FOR OWN ACTIONS

√ MANY SHORT-TERM MARITAL RELATIONSHIPS

√ JUVENILE DELINQUENCY

√ REVOCATION OF CONDITION RELEASE

√ CRIMINAL VERSATILITY

√ = The item applies to James Wood. No check mark indicates it does not apply or information was not available to make an informed decision.

According to Hare's Psychopathic Checklist, James Wood fits

every item on the checklist. He is a classic psychopathic, serial killer. The civil suit case was settled, and the amount and conditions were deemed confidential. That means, they were not told to me either. It is understood that an expert witness must be impartial and not have an interest in the outcome of a civil suit on which they have served.

CHAPTER TEN

~

ONE OF MANY - ROYCROFT VS. HAMMONS

Centrally located at the junction of I-35 and I-80, Des Moines is the state capitol of Iowa. It is a clean, busy city surrounded by miles and miles of lush green corn fields and bean fields. Thirty–six-year-old Patricia Lange, a white female, was staying alone in Room 732 at the Holiday Inn Executive Suites in Des Moines for ten days. She was in the process of looking for permanent housing as she went through training for her new IT job--a considerable advancement in her career.

This particular evening, Friday, August 22, 1993, she did her laundry and returned to her room. She had a boyfriend, but they did not go out that night. Sometime during the night, a man entered her room and viciously beat her and strangled her to death with ligatures made from the bedding and wire coat hangers. After she was dead, the perpetrator raped her, leaving his semen DNA on the bedspread, and on a sock underneath her body. That residue would ultimately close the door on Patricia Lange's murderer, just as he had closed the door on her room and on her life that night. It would take years, however, before the killer would be identified.

Patricia's body was found the next morning at 11am by a hotel housekeeper, and the police were immediately notified. During the investigation, Des Moines Police Detectives said that 150 semen stains were found on the bed-spread, which is not unusual. Bedspreads are sometimes only laundered every six months in hotels and blankets every three months. The semen stains get there not only from hotel guests who are having sex with someone or from masturbation. The semen stains also come from hotel employees having assignations and sexual encounters on the beds, often after the housekeeper has cleaned the room. In fact, it is sometimes the housekeeper who is having sex with a fellow employee or supervisor.

Since there was no sign of forcible entry, the police immediately thought the perpetrator was someone that Patricia knew or had let in, so her boyfriend became the key suspect. Employees and ex-employees were also questioned, and their DNA was taken. They were asked to write how, or why, this murder might have happened. One ex-employee, Donald Piper, wrote "key control." A match in his DNA was also found with the DNA in Patricia's room. He was the former building engineer, who had left two months earlier. He was questioned but said that his semen came from having an affair on that bed earlier, and he was home all night the night of the murder. His wife concurred that he was home all night. His wife claimed that since she also worked at the hotel at the front desk, his semen found in rooms, were from the two of them having sex in that room and other rooms, though she could not recall other specific room numbers.[40]

There was also corroborating evidence for his alibi from a housekeeper that she had an affair with Donald Piper in the hotel. The housekeeper presumably also had told Donald's wife Ruth, while she was working there at the front desk, that she (the housekeeper) was having an affair with Donald.

For four years, there were no more similar murders in Des Moines, and it was the perfect crime for Patricia's murderer, but then the perpetrator struck again in 1997, murdering Zurijeta Sakanovic. This time, the DNA tied Donald Piper to both victims. The article below shows Donald Piper in a photo and story taken from the *Des Moines Register* chronicling what happened next.[41]

Donald Piper

photo courtesy Des Moines Register

Full Name: Donald Arthur Piper
DOB: May 11, 1961
Charge: 1st degree murder
County: Polk, Dallas
City: West Des Moines, Clive
Current Status: Iowa State Penitentiary
Date of Crime: August 23, 1993, September 4, 1997
Tentative Discharge Date: Life
Victims: Patricia Lange, Zurijeta Sakanovic

Patricia Lange,
courtesy Des Moines Register

Patricia Lange was found murdered in her room at the University Park Holiday Inn in West Des Moines on Monday morning, August 23, 1993. She had a gag in her mouth and her hands were bound. Her top and bra had been pushed up to her shoulders and she had nothing on from the waist down except her tennis shoes and socks. It was determined that Patricia had been strangled with a wire coat hanger.

More than six years later, a match between DNA found at the murder scene and Donald Piper's DNA led authorities to charge Donald with Patricia's murder. Donald pleaded not guilty and claimed he was with his wife and other relatives during the weekend of August 21 and 22, and through the night of August 22 to August 23.

Donald's first trial ended in a mistrial in October 2000 when it was learned by the attorney for the first time that a portion of a vaginal swab taken from the victim was available for testing. A second trial ended 48 days later when the jury found Donald guilty of first-degree murder.

On September 4, 1997, Zurijeta Sakanovic, 21, a maid who did not speak English, was found stabbed and strangled at the Budgetel Inn in Clive, Iowa. Zurijeta, a Bosnian refugee, was found in room 309 of the hotel where she had worked for seven months, and was killed during her morning shift. She was found, partially nude, her wrists bound with white tape.

Donald, who had worked in the heating and cooling business, had access to the kind of tape used to render Zurijeta defenseless. He was already serving a life sentence for the murder of Patricia at the West Des Moines Holiday Inn. Patricia was also stabbed and strangled. Donald had quit his job as chief mechanical engineer at the hotel a month (or so) before Patricia was killed. He was convicted in 2001 for her murder.

DNA evidence helped convict Donald in both murders. His DNA was allegedly found in a small drop of blood on a blanket removed from the room where Zurijeta's body was found. [End article]

Authorities in Des Moines also investigated Donald in connection with the death of Mariana Redrovan, an Ecuadorian hotel maid at the West Des Moines Best Western Walnut Creek Inn. Authorities believe Mariana and Zurijeta's slayings were linked. Mariana was stabbed to death in January 1998. They have not, however, been able to prove this.[42]

After her murder, Zurijeta Sakanovic's family returned to Bosnia, from where they had earlier escaped the ravages of war, now saying: "It's safer in Bosnia than Des Moines".[43]

Piper Facing Second Murder Trial
Zurijeta Sakanovic Was Murdered In 1997[44]

Donald Piper plans to file an appeal in his first murder trial, meanwhile lawyers are preparing for his second murder trial. Piper was convicted Monday of the 1993 murder of Patricia Lange at the West Des Moines Holiday Inn. He faces another trial for the 1997 murder of Zurijeta Sakanovic scheduled for August.

Sakanovic was a 21-year-old housekeeper at the Budgetel Inn in Clive, Iowa. It's now called the Baymont Inn.

Someone found her body, and investigators soon found similarities between her murder case and the Patricia Lange case four years earlier, just across the Interstate at the Holiday Inn.

Donald Piper May Be A Serial Killer[45]

In court documents, prosecutors say both women were "identically positioned" in hotel rooms. Both women's hands were bound in front of their body. Lange with bed sheets, Sakanovic with electrical tape. And both women were strangled. More compelling, though, is the same type of evidence that jurors say led them to convict Piper in the Patricia Lange case: DNA. Court documents show that prosecutors say they have DNA evidence in this case linking Piper to the hotel room. Court papers say there is DNA testing "showing the Defendant's blood was found at the Sakanovic murder scene." Even some of the same DNA experts who testified in the Lange case could reappear in the Sakanovic case. And, like in the Lange case, Piper's defense lawyer has already questioned the DNA tests in the Sakanovic case.

Piper is also a suspect in a third hotel murder, though he's not been charged in that case. The victim is 15-year-old Mariana Redrovan. She was found murdered in January of 1998. She was a housekeeper at West Des Moines' Walnut Creek Inn. Months later, police issued a statement that the murders "may have been committed by the same person", discussed in the story below.[46]

Mariana Redrovan
Homicide
Mariana Redrovan
15 YOA
Case Number: 9800744
Walnut Creek Inn
West Des Moines, IA
Polk County
January 23, 1998
Case summary by Jody Ewing

On Friday, January 23, 1998, Mariana Redrovan, 15, was stabbed to death in a room at the West Des Moines Walnut Creek Inn where she worked as a housekeeper.

Redrovan, who was from Ecuador, was found (dead) by her supervisor in a guest room.

Polk County in Iowa

Des Moines in Polk County

The deputy director of the INS office in Omaha, Neb., said Redrovan was employed illegally at the Walnut Creek Inn because she did not have proper documentation to enter the country and worked more hours than the law allows for a 15-year-old.[47] The hotel's general manager, said Redrovan presented a driver's license and a social security card with a last name of "Prieto" and an age of 17 when she was hired nine months earlier.[End Article].

Patricia Lange's murderer was in fact found to be Donald Piper, who was 32 years old at the time, and had left the job a month or more before, with the master keys. The night of Patricia's murder, Donald Piper's mother-in-law had come to town and was staying overnight with him, his wife, and children. He quietly passed her, his wife and kids, as he went out that night, headed to the Holiday Inn. In interviews, however, his wife would claim that he was at home that whole night; thus, providing an alibi for him that could have saved the lives of the three other women, that he is believed to have killed after that. Piper was tried and found guilty in his first murder trial of Patricia Lange. After an appeal, and a retrial, he was again found guilty. He was then tried and found guilty of the murder of Zurijeta Sakanovic. An appeal was also filed on October 15, 2003 by Donald Piper on the Sakanovic trial, with evidence presented and shown below. [48]

Donald Piper's Appeal

Background Facts: Sakanovic died on September 4, 1997. Her body was discovered by a co-employee, Tanya Fast, in a guest room of the Clive Budgetel Inn, where both worked in housekeeping. Fast found Sakanovic lying on the side of a bed. Sakanovic's pants and underwear had been removed, and her shirt and bra were pushed up exposing her breasts. Sakanovic's hands were bound in front of her with white tape. A subsequent medical exam indicated she had been strangled and stabbed multiple times.

Piper was implicated in Sakanovic's murder because he matched the description of a man Fast saw exit an elevator and hurriedly leave the hotel shortly before she found Sakanovic's body. Fast subsequently identified Piper in a photo array with eighty-five percent certainty as the man she saw leaving the hotel. Other evidence implicating Piper included a videotape from a neighboring convenience store depicting a white van resembling that which Piper drove for his employer, Accurate Mechanical Contractors, at a stoplight near the hotel. Additionally the tape used to bind Sakanovic's hands was of a type used by mechanical contractors and not generally sold at retail. DNA tests of a blood stain found on the bedspread of the guest room matched a DNA sample taken from Piper.

Testimony. Allen Beery reported he had received a catalog addressed to "Donald Piper or current resident." As the current resident, Beery opened the catalog, which depicted women in bondage in sexual poses. Robert Ellis testified that Piper loaned him a videotape which depicted sex acts and people in bondage. The court determined the evidence was relevant because the attack on Sakanovic included a sexual component and she was found with her wrists bound. The evidence showed Piper had some knowledge of bondage techniques. The court concluded the relevance of the evidence was not outweighed by the danger of unfair prejudice. We find no abuse of discretion in the court's determination that the evidence was relevant to a legitimate issue in dispute, which was whether Piper was the person who had bound Sakanovic's wrists and then killed her. The testimony that Piper had possession of materials depicting people in bondage showed that he had knowledge of bondage techniques. Additionally, insofar as the crime was sexual in nature, the evidence was relevant to show Piper had possession of materials showing people in bondage in sexual poses.

[End Court Papers]

It is possible that he is also responsible for the murder of 33 year old Julie Davis of Marion, Iowa who was killed August 28, 1997 at her office near downtown Des Moines, creating the following timeline for serial killer Donald Piper:[49, 50, 51, 52]

Donald Piper's Murder Timeline

April 27, 1987. Donald Piper started work at the hotel in question.

June 22, 1993. Donald Piper left his job, after six years, as maintenance chief —two months before Patricia is slain. He went to another mechanical firm as a service technician, until he was fired six years later.

August 16, 1993. Patricia Lange, 36, is found dead in her room at the West Des Moines Holiday Inn, where she had been staying for ten days. She had been strangled and raped.

December, 1993. Police received a Crime Stopper call

identifying Donald Piper as a suspect.

August 28, 1997. Julie Davis, 33, was killed at her office near downtown Des Moines. [Piper was suspected but never charged in this case].

Sept. 4, 1997. Zurijeta Sakanovic, 21, a maid, was found stabbed and strangled, at the Budgetel Inn in Clive, Iowa.

Jan. 16, 1998. Mariana Redrovan, 15, a maid, was found stabbed at Best Western Walnut Creek in West Des Moines, Iowa. [Piper was never tried in this case].

October 8, 1999. Piper was fired by a mechanical company, after six years, because of his constant surveillance by police, over the past six months, which the company said interfered with their operations.

January 22, 2000. Donald Piper, 38, was arrested and charged with the first degree murder of Patricia Lange.

June 4, 2001. Piper was convicted of the murder of Patricia Lange.

The combined timeline above tells the story of the actions of serial murderer Donald Piper. As a result of the convictions of the murders of both Lange and Sakanovic, Piper is now serving two life-sentences without the possibility of parole in maximum security in an Iowa State Prison. Iowa does not have the death sentence, so he will have a lot of time to think about the time-line and his actions.

The Civil Suit

The murder of Patricia Lange occurred in 1993, but the civil suit against the Holiday Inn Hotel was not filed until 8 years later in 2001. I was hired to defend the hotel, but the first issue addressed was the late filing of civil case against the hotel:

Defendant filed for a motion for summary judgment (MSJ in 2001). The basis for the MSJ was that the civil case was brought so many years after the crime. The reason, given by plaintiff, was that plaintiff did not know until the police advised the attorneys that the real perpetrator was Donald Piper--a stranger to Patricia--not a known person to whom she allowed entrance. As a result of this finding, the complaint, described in Footnote 1 of the Court's ruling on the MSJ, was as follows:[53]

Specifically, the complaint alleges that the University Park Holiday Inn ("Holiday Inn") breached its duty of care owed to Patricia Lange in the following particulars: (a) in negligently hiring Donald Piper ("Piper") without conducting a proper background check; (b) in negligently retaining Piper as chief engineer despite the fact that the Holiday Inn knew or should have known about his criminal history, his propensity for sexually harassing female employees, and his propensity for physically abusing female employees; (c) in negligently allowing Piper access to master keys in spite of its failure to conduct a background check; (d) in negligently allowing Piper access to master keys and failing to limit his access to the hotel while he was employed there and in negligently failing to limit Piper's access to the Holiday Inn and master keys following his "resignation", all in spite of the fact that Holiday Inn knew or should have known about Piper's criminal history, his propensity for sexually harassing women, and his propensity for sexually abusing women; (e) in negligently failing to situate Patricia Lange, a single female traveling alone, on a lower floor near an elevator in conformity with the written security guidelines of the Holiday Inn; (f) in negligently failing to provide proper security; and (g) in failing to act as a reasonable innkeeper under the circumstances then and there existing. These last three claims, termed "negligent security/innkeeping claims", are the subject of the present motion.

[End MSJ]

The MSJ was denied with this statement from the court:[54]

Where the issue of limitations involves determinations [of when a claim begins to accrue], summary judgment cannot be granted unless the evidence is so clear that there is no genuine factual issue and the determinations can be made as a matter of law. Hildebrandt v. Allied Corp., 839 F.2d 396, 399 (8th Cir. 1989). Defendants concede that there is a factual question as to when Plaintiff could have learned of Piper's connection to the murder. Where the determination of when the cause of action accrued involves a material factual dispute, summary judgment is not appropriate. Hines v. A. O. Smith Harvestore

> Products, Inc., 880 F.2d 995, 998 (8th Cir. 1989). [End MSJ Ruling]

One role I had in the defense for the hotel was to have the parties involved consider the facts in *historical context*, not from the standards for security nearly a decade later, when the civil case was being considered. Advances had been made in the 1990s, particularly with regard to security cameras, key control, and background screening for employees. I argued that you could not take a security template from 2001 and apply it to 1993. Accordingly, I offered opinions on 1) foreseeability and 2) standard of care, in the context of 1993, the year in which Patricia Lange was murdered. I based foreseeability on the following factors in my defense of the hotel where Patricia Lange was murdered:

1) **Crime in the area.** In 1993, with the exception of this case, there were NO murders and only five rapes in all of West Des Moines, according to the FBI Uniform Crime Reports for that year.[55]

2) **Prior crimes at the location.** There had not been any homicides, robberies, or rapes at this hotel, based either on internal hotel incident report or police calls to the location.

3) **The unusual nature of this crime.** Rape/Murders are a very rare crime. 1993, nationwide, there were only 116 rape/murders. Stranger rape/murder is also very rare. In 1993, only 32 rape/murders were by strangers, and 34 were by acquaintances. The rest were either domestic or unknown. Of the 104,806 rapes in 1993, only 1% ended in murder.[56]

4) **The unusual nature of the perpetrator.** This type of perpetrator is typically a young (20s to 30s) white male, who is employed and married; thus masking his true nature.

Standard of Care

No laws, codes, or regulations at the city, county, or federal level, in operation in 1993, were broken by Hammons Hotel at the time of this incident.

- There were no written, published standards for the hospitality industry in 1993.
- Surveillance cameras were not, in 1993, a standard of the industry.
- Hotels were moving toward the use of electronic keys, but they were not the standard for the industry in 1993.
- Some hotels had security guards, and this one did. Some hotels conducted employment background check, but there were more limitations on what could be discovered, and it is not clear that his perpetrator had priors that would have been discovered in 1993.
- There was no standard on the placement of single females in hotels in 1993.
- Sexual harassment in the workplace, and how to deal with it, was a relatively new concept in 1993. There were not published standards for responding to it in 1993.

Further, there was no evidence of how the perpetrator gained access, though it was eventually assumed that it was with Piper's master key set. With the police evidence, or his admission, there is no causation that be established between his employment, hiring, firing, or retention, his access to keys while he was an employee and this murder. He may have gained entrance to her rooms, as any perpetrator who has not been an employee can gain access to a room, through ruse, following her in; knocking and being admitted, with a claim of needing to check on something in her room.

In fact, Piper was charged with the subsequent murders of two other women in hotels, where he had not been an employee and did not have access to keys.

Hare's checklist of psychopathy is shown below to compare it with what is known about Donald Piper.[57] Below, I analyze his psychopathy, based on the evidence in the criminal and civil cases.

Donald Piper Psychopathy Check List

√ GLIB and SUPERFICIAL CHARM

√ GRANDIOSE SELF-WORTH

√ NEED FOR STIMULATION or PRONENESS TO BOREDOM

√ PATHOLOGICAL LYING

√ CONNING AND MANIPULATIVENESS√

√ LACK OF REMORSE OR GUILT

√ SHALLOW

√ CALLOUSNESS and LACK OF EMPATHY

 PARASITIC LIFESTYLE

√ POOR BEHAVIORAL CONTROLS

√ PROMISCUOUS SEXUAL BEHAVIOR

EARLY BEHAVIOR PROBLEMS

√ LACK OF REALISTIC, LONG-TERM GOALS

IMPULSIVITY

IRRESPONSIBILITY

√FAILURE TO ACCEPT RESPONSIBILITY FOR OWN ACTIONS

MANY SHORT-TERM MARITAL RELATIONSHIPS

JUVENILE DELINQUENCY

REVOCATION OF CONDITION RELEASE

CRIMINAL VERSATILITY

√ = The item applies to Donald Piper. No check mark indicates it does not apply or information was not available to make an informed decision.

From what we know of Donald Piper, he fits many of the categories of psychopathy above, but not all; whereas James Wood fit all of them. Unlike some serial killers, Piper's life was normal on the surface--married, with children, and he maintained steady employment, years at a time. What fits for him, however, is his charm, promiscuous sexual activity, manipulation, cunning, and lying, and he did not admit to or take responsibility for the murders. By either the FBI definition (3 murders) or the Department of Justice definition (2 murders), shown below, Donald Piper is a serial killer:[58]

The official FBI definition, taken from the FBI Crime Classification Manual, from 1992: "Three or more separate events in three or more separate locations with an emotional cooling-off period between homicides."

This definition stresses three important elements:

1.   Quantity. There have to be at least three murders.
2.   Place. The murders have to occur at different locations
3.   Time. There has to be a "cooling-off period"-an interval between the murders that can last anywhere from several hours to several years.

However, there are several problems with this FBI definition – it's too broad and overly narrow. These flaws are rectified in another, more flexible one formulated by the National Institutes of Justice, which many authorities regard as a more accurate description:

Serial Killer Definition

A series of two or more murders, committed as separate events, usually, but not always, by one offender acting alone. The crimes may occur over a period of time ranging from hours to years. Quite often the motive is psychological, and the offender's behavior and the physical evidence observed at the crime scenes will reflect sadistic, sexual overtones. [NIJ Definition]

The civil case, for which I was hired for the defense, and related to the murder of Patricia Lange did not go to trial and was settled. Thus, ended the civil suit in this case, but the story of a serial killer never ends because of the victims' families who live with the loss for the rest of their lives.

CHAPTER ELEVEN

~

FOLLOW THE LEADER –
BURNS VS. HUNTINGTON MALL

Samantha Burns, a slender, beautiful, 19-year-old white female, with long dark hair, had met her aunt at the mall at 5:30 the evening of Monday, November 11, 2002 (Veterans Day) to help her aunt get a gift for her niece. She and her aunt separated on the lower floor of the Huntington Mall in Barboursville, West Virginia. Samantha went out the back door of the mall around 6:30 pm--dark by then--and her aunt went out the front door of the mall. When Samantha reached her car, she was taken hostage by two of the most evil men in the country, and she has never been seen again. This is the poster about her disappearance that night.[59]

West Virginia State Police Missing Person Report

Vital Statistics at Time of Disappearance

- Missing Since: November 11, 2002 from Huntington, West Virginia
- Classification: Endangered Missing
- Date of Birth: April 23, 1983
- Age at time of disappearance: 19
- Height: 5'4"
- Weight: 110 lbs.
- Hair Color: Brown
- Eye Color: Hazel
- Race: White
- Gender: Female
- Distinguishing Characteristics: Chicken pox scars on the right side of forehead. Tattoo of a butterfly on lower back, pierced ears and pierced tongue.
- Clothing: Orange fuzzy sweater with a tank top underneath, low-cut rider jeans that flared at the bottom, light tan suede mule shoes and leopard print purse.
- Jewelry: Diamond stud earrings, a heart-shaped ring with a diamond in the center of the heart.
- AKA: "Sam", "Sammy"
- NCIC Number: M-772839413
- Case Number: 5200-24308

Details of Disappearance

Samantha Burns was last seen by her aunt at the Huntington Mall in Barboursville, WV, at 6:30 on the evening of November 11, 2002. Later, at 9:45 p.m. that evening, Burns used her cellular phone to call her mother and said she had been visiting friends at Marshall University Court Yard Apartments but was coming home. Burns lived in East Hamlin, West Virginia. She never arrived there and has never been heard from again. The call to her mother was the last one Burns made on her phone. After her disappearance the phone was discovered to be turned off, which is uncharacteristic of Burns.

At 3:30 a.m. on November 12, Burns' 1999 burgundy Chevrolet Cavalier with a tiger sticker in the back window on the driver's side and a license plate numbered 5X9326 was found abandoned in Wayne County, West Virginia. The vehicle was discovered in a secluded area at German Ridge and Haneys Branch Roads, near the Cabell-Wayne county line. It had been set on fire; when the police found it, it was still burning. There was no sign of Burns near the vehicle.

In July 2005, Chadrick Fulks and Brandon Basham pleaded guilty to a federal charge of carjacking resulting in death to avoid a possible death sentence. Basham and Fulks had escaped from the Hopkins County (Ky.) Jail in November 2002. They have said that they carjacked Burns shortly thereafter and killed her, though her body has not been found. They are currently on death row for another killing, that of Alice Donovan from South Carolina. Donovan's remains have not been found. [Donovan's remains were later found]. If you have any information concerning this case, please contact: West Virginia State Police. [End Police Poster]

Basham (P1) tells the story this way. He says that Fulks liked the way Burns' car looked, so when she was getting in her car, he instructed Basham to jump out of the van they were in and take the car. He forced Burns into her car and instructed her to follow the van. Basham stated that he and Burns followed Fulks in the van. The Victim (V) was sexually assaulted, he says, and not shot or stabbed, and her body was placed in the river. (FBI, p. 247).

The following description is taken from Fulks (P2):

> The Victim (V) was abducted from behind the mall in the parking lot by Basham (P1). Basham forced her to drive to the front of the mall where Fulks was located. Basham drove the V's car, and the victim was handcuffed, raped, and murdered by Basham, according to Fulks (FBI, p. 49).

The evidence in the case confirmed the following: The victim's car was later found burned, and her body has never been found. Numerous attempts, some successful, were made to use her ATM card, and images are captured on surveillance tape from the bank(s). She had called her mother at approximately 9:30 PM saying she was on her way home, according to her mother and cell phone records. The two perpetrators went on to commit a similar crime in South Carolina and attempted another similar abduction in Ashland, KY. Both of the perpetrators had prior criminal records, they were escapees from a jail in

Kentucky, and they were embarked on a multi-state crime spree.

Robbery appeared to be the primary motive, since both Fulks and Basham say they were looking for money. They took her car initially, and they had stolen other cars. They also stole her ATM card and used it at various locations to obtain money and stole her diamond ring. There is also evidence that in addition to their camouflage clothes, they had gloves, masks, and handcuffs. This crime included robbery, rape, homicide, and arson, all characteristics of an indiscriminate felony murder. It was also part of a much larger, extended crime spree being carried out by these two perpetrators beginning with their break from jail as discussed below.

I was hired by the Huntington Mall to defend the civil case. I held the opinions given below with a reasonable degree of scientific and professional certainty, based on foreseeability and the unusual nature of the crime and perpetrators, as outlined below. I had the benefit in the analysis of this crime to have over 1,000 pages of criminal trial and a 50-year social work-up was available on both individuals and their families. The crime occurred in 2002, and this is the report below that I wrote in the first person and prepared for the defense, with references and citations given within the report and not in the endnotes.

Foreseeability

It is my opinion that this crime at this location was not foreseeable based on the unusual nature of the crime and the unusual nature of the perpetrators.

The Unusual Nature of the Crime

There are a number of characteristics of this crime that make it unusual and therefore unforeseeable. One is that females are far less likely to be assaulted by strangers than males are. Another is that homicide in a rape is very rare. Another factor is that murder in a robbery is not common. Further, resistance is usually the main reason for injury and death. These factors are discussed below.

1) Female Victimization

It is unusual for females to be victims of assault by strangers. According to the Bureau of Justice Statistics (BJS), males experience violent crime at a rate 42% greater than females and are robbed at a rate 159% greater than females.

2) Death in a rape

Injury and death in a rape are rare. The Bureau of Justice Statistics (BJS) reports in 2002, that most sexual assault victims were not injured (83%). Death is even more rare. In the year of this crime, of all the 14,054 homicides in the nation, only 40 were females that were killed in a rape-related homicide (FBI).

3) Death in a robbery

Death in a robbery is also uncommon for a female. In the year of the crime, of the 14,054 homicides in the country, 1,092 were robbery-related, but only 156 of those were females. Males are much more likely to be victims of robbery-related homicides than are females. Injuries in robberies are rare, and death is rarer. According to the BJS, in two-thirds of robberies, there is no injury. In fact, according to BJS, in three out of four of all violent crimes, no one is injured.

4) Resistance in a Robbery

When death or injury occurs in a robbery, they are usually as a result of resistance. In fact, active resistance was found to account for 82 percent of commercial robbery killings, and victims who resisted were forty-nine times more likely to be killed than those who cooperated, according to a Chicago study by Zimring and Zuehl, cited in my article on "Set Your Sights" in *Security Management*. The point of robbery training is to train people to give up the money without resistance

Commercial robberies of cashiers, for example, have less injury because employees are trained to give up the money and not resist. Clerks report that they say such things as "Take it. It's not mine anyway." Robberies of individuals, such as street muggings, have more injury than commercial robberies because individuals are less likely to be willing to give up their possessions, especially their purse or their car. Resistance was not likely the motive in this crime.

5) Crime Spree

According to the *Crime Classification Manual*, this crime most closely fits the classification of an *indiscriminate felony murder*, described below with excerpts from pages 64-66. The *Manual* was authored by former FBI profiler John Douglas and associates (1992) to standardize terminology and formally classify the critical characteristics of the perpetrators and victims of violent crime. It identifies for investigators the clues and crime scene indicators common to each of the major violent crimes and is used by investigators, prosecutors, mental health professionals, criminal justice and correctional institution personnel, and criminologists. This crime fits the classification of indiscriminate felony murder.

---

108.   Felony Murder
Property crime (robbery, burglary) is the primary motivation for felony murder, with murder the secondary motivation. During the commission of a violent crime, a homicide occurs. There are two types of felony murder: indiscriminate felony murder (108.01) and situational felony murder (108.02).

108.01. Indiscriminate felony murder
An indiscriminate felony murder is a homicide without a specific victim in mind.
Defining characteristics
• **Victimology.** The victim is a potential witness to the crime and appears to be no apparent threat to the offender. They may offer no resistance but are killed anyway. The victim is one of opportunity.
  • **Staging.** If staging is present, arson frequently is used

---

to conceal the felony murder. If the motive seems to be monetary, investigators should require a sexual assault examination of the victim.

- **Common Forensic Findings**. Most often the manner of death involves the use of firearms. There can be blunt-force trauma and/or battery present. There also may be evidence of restraints used (handcuffs, gags, blindfolds, etc). Sexual assault also may occur.

- **Investigative Considerations**. It is important to focus on this as a robbery and not as a murder. The offender is usually a youthful male with criminal history (history of auto theft appears especially prevalent).

Search Warrant Suggestions. Look for the victim's possessions, such as wallets, watches, jewelry and the perpetrators' possessions, including ski mask, stocking mask etc., and drugs or evidence of drug use.

Serial murder is estimated to account for less than 2% of all homicides in this country in any given year (Jenkins, 1994 in Skrapec, at p. 11), and spree murder is even rarer; thus, the spree murder is even more unforeseeable than a serial murder or other murders by strangers. The *Crime Classification Manual* defines *spree murder* below, with excerpts from p. 94 of the Manual.

Spree Murder

Spree murder involves multiple killings of at least two or more at two or more locations without any appreciable cooling-off period between murders. The killer usually suffers from one or more mental disorders (i.e., paranoia, psychosis, depressive disorders, etc.). However, the killer moves from one location to another during his killing spree, rather than barricading himself in one location as does the mass murderer. The duration of the spree can be brief (minutes) or much longer (weeks and months). As a rule, the spree is of shorter duration. This type of offender is usually mission oriented and demonstrates no escape plan. He most often is killed by responding police or kills himself in a final act of desperation. Occasionally, he is captured to stand trial. When this occurs,

---

the offender often admits his crimes by pleading guilty or by pleading not guilty by reason of insanity.

Additional definitions of spree murder come from Holmes and Holmes *Murder in America* (2nd Edition) 2001, Sage Publications, in defining spree murder as three or more victims and further saying that it takes place within a 30-day time period and typically is accompanied by a felony, such as robbery (p. 35). Fulks, when told that Hawkins was alive, was surprised to learn that, so he apparently thought they had killed three people at that point. (FBI Investigation).

Regarding the number of victims, Ressler, Burgess and Douglas in *Sexual Homicide* (1988, Lexington Books) on p. 138 classify spree killers as having two or more victims, and serial killers having three or more. Further, they point out that there are two or more locations for the spree killer and no real cooling off period, certainly not one of weeks, months, or years, as a serial killer generally has. Ressler et. al., at p. 139, point out that a spree murderer is not concerned with who their victims are, they will kill anyone who comes in contact with them. This is in contrast to a serial murderer who usually selects a type of victim. At p. 140, they note that a spree murderer has oftentimes been identified and is being closely pursued by law enforcement. He knows he will be caught and is anticipating the coming confrontation with police. This was the case with Basham and Fulks, with repeated testimony from Severance and Roddy (the girls with them) that Basham especially was always thinking they were being pursued. The actions of these two perpetrators are characteristic of *spree murder* in that they killed at least two people at two locations within a few days of each other. They had mental disorders, and both were reportedly using drugs from childhood and during the spree. Even before the murders of Burns and Donovan, the pair was on a crime spree covering a large geographical area over a relatively short period of time, according to the crime spree route and map shown below, with the locations that they stayed each night.

Crime Spree Route
Fulks & Basham
November 4, 2002-November 20, 2002
7 states-17 days

1.Madisonville, KY	Mon, Nov 4, 2002
2.Hanson, KY	Tues, Nov 5, 2002
3.Portage, IL	Wed & Thurs, Nov 6 & 7, 2002
4.Sturgis, MI	Fri, Nov 8, 2002
5.Goshen, IN	Sat, Nov 9, 2002
6.Piketon, OH	Sun, Nov 10, 2002
7.Kenova/Huntington, WV	Mon, Nov 11, 2002
8.Conway, SC	Tues & Wed, Nov 12 & 13, 2002
9.Myrtle Beach, SC	Thurs, Nov 14, 2002
10.Huntington, WV	Fri & Sat, Nov 15 & 16
11.Ashland, KY	Sun, Nov 17, 2002
12.Goshen, IN	Mon, Tues & Wed, Nov 18, 19 & 20

Crime Spree Route
Fulks & Basham
November 4, 2002 - November 20, 2002
7 States-17 Days

1. Madisonville, KY Mon, Nov. 4, 2002
2. Hanson, KY Tues, Nov. 5, 2002
3. Portage, IN Wed, & Thurs. Nov. 6 & 7, 2002
4. Sturgis, MI Fri, Nov. 8, 2002
5. Goshen, IN Sat, Nov. 9, 2002
6. Piketon, OH Sun, Nov. 10, 2002
7. Kenova, WV Mon, Nov. 11, 2002
8. Conway, SC Tues. & Wed, Nov. 12 & 13, 2002
9. Myrtle Beach, SC Thurs, Nov. 14, 2002
10. Huntington, WV Fri. & Sat, Nov. 15 & 16, 2002
11. Ashland, KY Sun, Nov. 17, 2002
12. Goshen, IN Mon, Tues. & Wed. Nov. 18,19 & 20, 2002

The crimes they committed are described in the time-line below taken from the West Virginia State Police investigation, by date, by type of crime, and by location. Their 17-day crime spree lasted from November 4, 2002 to November 20, 2002, slightly over two weeks. They covered seven states and thousands of miles, leaving fear, death, and carnage in their wake. CNN reported on 11/18/02 that the police were officially calling it a *crime spree*. These were three significant events that took place before the spree.

September 17, 2001. Basham is booked into Hopkins County Detention Center in Madisonville, KY, so he has been there for over a year at the time of the escape. Basham had escaped from this jail before. He was there this time to serve time for burglary and forgery. His prior charges include forgery (of his father's checks) and selling prescription drugs.

Monday, August 26, 2002. Fulks is booked into Hopkins County Detention Center in Madisonville, KY to await trial for probation violation. His prior charges include fraudulent use of a credit card, possession of a handgun by a felon, theft of license plates and street robbery. In mid-October he is placed with Fulks as his cellmate. Basham had difficulty keeping cellmates because he pestered them, and they requested new cell mates.

Sunday, November 3, 2002. Kentucky State Police serve Fulks with an indictment charging him with first degree abuse of a child aged twelve years or younger (Miles).

Crime Spree Timeline for Chadrick Fulks and Brandon Basham

November 4, 2002 - November 20, 2002

Monday, November 4, 2002.
With help from a female prison guard, Fulks and Basham escape at approximately 8 PM. She had helped them by providing pliers, a razor, leaving them alone and unsupervised in the yard and (not) watching the camera at the time of their escape—a camera that they had moved

---

with a basketball.

Tuesday, November 5, 2002.
Fulks and Basham abduct Hawkins in Hanson, KY; tie him to a tree in Indiana, and steal his 1989 GMC truck.

Wednesday, November 6, 2002.
Fulks and Basham show up at Tina Severance and Andrea Roddy's home in Portage, IL in early morning; all four check into the Sands Motel. Tina is Fulks' girlfriend.

Thursday, November 7, 2002.
They all four spend the day at the Sands Motel in Portage, IL.

Friday, November 8, 2002.
They all four drive Tina's Ford van and Jeep to her friend's (Robert Talsma); Tina and Andrea lure Talsma away while Fulks and Basham burglarize his house, stealing four hand-guns and his check book and credit cards; drive van to Sturgis, MI and stay at a motel with the two women.

Saturday, November 9, 2002.
Fulks and Basham buy clothing at a K-Mart; drive to Fulks' brother's in Goshen, IN with the two women.

Sunday, November 10, 2002.
All four drive to Piketon, OH; stay in motel; buy camouflage clothing at Wal-Mart; party with drugs with teenagers they met there.

Monday, November 11, 2002.
All four arrive in the morning at Hollywood Motel in Kenova, WV. At 6:30 pm approximately, Fulks and Basham allegedly carjack, abduct, rob, rape and murder Samantha Burns from the Huntington Mall in Barboursville, WV.

Tuesday, November 12, 2002.
Fulks and Basham arrive at the Hollywood Motel between 2 and 3 am, after burning Burns' car on deserted road; drive to Conway, SC and check into a Lake Shore Motel in Conway, SC. Burns' burned out car

was found at 3 that morning in WV.

Wednesday, November 13, 2002.
All four stay at the Lake Shore Motel in Conway, SC.

Thursday, November 14, 2002.
All four check in at the Beach Walk Motel in Myrtle Beach, SC; Fulks and Basham attempt to burglarize a trailer house but are chased off and shot at; they steal a white pickup from a farm and drive it to Wal-Mart in Conway, SC. There, they carjack and abduct Alice Donovan in her BMW at 2:37 PM, leaving the stolen white pick-up there; drive north into NC and are last seen near Shallotte, NC; both perpetrators rape victim; kill her; and drive back to Myrtle Beach, presumably without Donovan. Fulks and Basham pack up and leave in Donovan's BMW and drive to Huntington, WV, leaving Severance and Roddy stranded in SC.

Friday, November 15, 2002.
Fulks and Basham arrive at Beth McGuffin's house in Huntington, WV. Beth is an old childhood friend of Fulks. Severance reports her van missing. Fulks and Basham use Donovan's ATM card in Raleigh, NC at 12:21 AM. McGuffin and Basham become sexually involved.

Saturday, November 16, 2002.
They remained in Huntington, WV at Beth McGuffin's house.

Sunday, November 17, 2002.
Basham arrested at Ashland, KY Town Center mall after attempting to carjack a mother and daughter at Wal-Mart, ending in a shoot-out with a police officer.

Monday, November 18, 2002.
Fulks drives through OH to his brother Ronnie's house in Goshen, IN; chased in OH by Highway Patrol near Marion, OH after being spotted in a rest area but not caught.

Tuesday, November 19, 2002.
Beth McGuffin calls the FBI in Huntington, WV. Fulks is still in Goshen, IN.

> **Wednesday, November 20, 2002.**
> Fulks is arrested in Goshen, IN; his brother Ron and girlfriend are
> with him after hiding Donovan's BMW in a barn.

As can be seen from the crime spree timeline and crime spree route, their crime spree took them through seven states over a period of 17 days and included a myriad of crimes, including jail escape, larceny, theft, abduction, kidnapping, carjacking, arson, murder, rape, assault, aggravated assault, robbery, and others. The crimes perpetrated against Burns are believed to have included abduction, kidnapping, carjacking, arson, murder, rape, assault, aggravated assault, and robbery.

In closing arguments of the criminal trial, the prosecutor Mr. Gasser describes the crime spree as follows at Volume XXI, beginning at p. 92. "Chad goes from Madisonville, Kentucky; through Evansville; to Portage, where he arms himself with guns; to Huntington, West Virginia, where the rape, kidnapping, murder, body disposal of Samantha Burns; down to Myrtle Beach, South Carolina and Conway, where Alice Donovan is abducted, carjacked, raped, and murdered; up into Winnabow; back to South Carolina; enroute back to Raleigh, drives on back to Huntington, West Virginia, where he does his thing, where he parties; and when he goes up to Marion, Ohio, and the high-speed chase almost killing trooper Malo; and, back to his brother's house, where he was arrested."

In an article entitled "Defining Serial Murder" found in the *Journal of Police and Criminal Psychology*, 2001, Vol 16, #2, on p. 14, Candice Skrapec describes spree murder in this way: "In yet another category of *multicide*, spree murder, victims are killed within a relatively narrow interval of time such as hours, days, or weeks. The incidents of murder are part of a criminal agenda carried out over a limited period of time. In this sense, the murders are contiguous—part of an unbroken sequence of events. There is generally a clear point of onset and a decided end to the crimes. We have long talked of offenders going on crime or murder sprees as described below, by Skrapec.

In Salt Lake City in 1966, Myron Lance and Walter Kelbach killed five people over a period of five days on a crime spree that included homosexual rape, robbery, and murder." The crime spree at issue in this case has many similarities to one by Lance (age 25) and Kelbach (age 28) in Salt Lake City in 1966 (See *Serial Killer Central*). Kelbach and Lance shared a fondness for inflicting pain and were both abusive homosexuals. They first robbed a service station attendant, drove him to the desert and raped, stabbed, and killed him. The next day, they kidnapped another male night attendant at a filling station, raped, stabbed and killed him. Three days later on December 21, they changed their modus operandi (MO) and switched to a taxi driver. They robbed him, and then shot and killed him. They went directly to a tavern and shot a customer in the head, robbed the cash register, and shot at several others, killing two of them. They fled on foot and were captured at a roadblock several hours later. They were later convicted and sentenced to death, but their penalties were commuted to life in prison, and they are theoretically eligible for parole.

Judge Robert Chambers in the sentencing hearing for Chad Fulks on June 30, 2005, at p. 54, characterizes it as a crime spree, when he says: 'What you did after you left her on a crime spree down through South Carolina with other victims was the epitome of evil". The same judge, in his sentencing of Brandon Basham on July 25, 2005 at p. 46 says: This was a random abduction of Samantha. And the events that followed demonstrated how evil and cold-hearted you and Mr. Fulks could be." This crime is unusual in and of itself and unusual in Huntington. The Huntington Police Department was quoted in the *Herald Dispatch* on 11/9/02 as saying: "It's very rare for a juvenile to be abducted around here." (P. 333 of WVSP).

The Unusual Nature of the Perpetrators

The criminological theories that apply to Fulks and Basham include four in particular, those of the *irrational actor* theory, the *coaching* theory, the *rotten social background* theory and *psychopathy*. From the information provided below, it can be seen that Fulks and Basham were psychopaths by all indications. They both had rotten social backgrounds, as seen from their childhood, with difficult circumstances and violence. They saw violence, they experienced violence, and they were coached into violence. Their psychopathy led them to be irrational actors engaging in a crime spree and ending with indiscriminate felony homicides, as outlined on the chart below.

The Making of a Psychopathic Killer

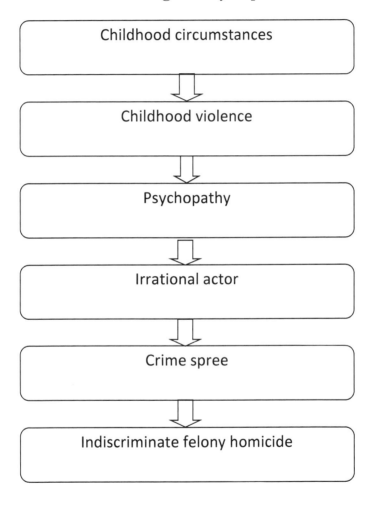

Irrational Actor Theory

In criminology, it is commonly accepted that deterrence measures can only deter the *rational actor* from committing a crime because it is virtually impossible to guard against the actions of an *irrational actor*. A *rational actor* can also be thought of as a *reasoning criminal*. An *irrational actor* is one who is impaired, for some reason, due to drugs, alcohol, mental illness, or judgment. Cornish & Clarke in *The Reasoning Criminal* discuss the characteristics of a reasoning criminal, and Feeney in a separate chapter in the same book at 66-67 notes that if someone is loaded on drugs or alcohol, it makes them irrational actors.

Ressler et. al. at p. 144 note that the disorganized offender may be mentally ill or have distorted thinking (similar to the irrational actor discussed above). Drugs and alcohol, as well as panic and stress, are additional factors that may affect the perpetrator and his behavior. These were behaviors exhibited by Basham and Fulks. Fox and Levin in *Extreme Killings* (2005, Sage Publications) say at p. 146 that disorganized killers are not mobile, or drive an old car or do not own one. This was notable about Basham because frequent references were made to his lack of ability to drive and lack of desire to drive--unusual for a young male living in a rural area. Brandon's sister Charlotte said he never took the test and never drove (SC Trial 21-82). The killer is also sometimes identifying with whoever tortured him, and is now the one in power (Fox & Levin) at p. 101, as when a man kills a woman who reminds him of his abusive mother. Both Fulks' and Basham's mothers abused them.

The theory of the *rational actor* stems from the belief that one needs to understand not only the criminal and his motivations, but how he selects his targets. If he uses a process of rational decision-making in selecting his targets, then he is considered a *rational actor*. If he does not use a process of reasoning in the selection of his targets, then he is considered an *irrational actor*. There is no indication going into the event that Basham or Fulks intended to do any more than their usual break-ins. And there is no indication from their interviews with the police or FBI that they paid any particular attention to security measures or had a concern about being caught. Christopher Staten, of the

Barboursville Police Department said in a statement on p. 12 that "When somebody decides that they're going to do something of that nature, they're going to do it, and unless you're right there on top of it, you are not going to be able to deter that."

Coaching Theory

Sociologist Lonnie Athens' theory of coaching is described on p. 15 in *Teenage Robbers*. For a child to become a violent criminal, three factors are needed: They need to: 1) see violence, 2) experience violence, and 3) be coached in violence. In the paragraphs below, we will see how Fulks and Basham experienced all three variables. This helps to answer the question that people often ask about why some children can grow up with a bad social environment and turn out okay and others do not. It may be explained by the coaching theory and further explained by the fact that one strong person in such an environment, which could be a member of the family, or the school, the juvenile justice system, or other social institution, can prevent future violence. But with that failing, the combination of factors, including the psychopathy to be discussed, cast the die.

Rotten Social Background Theory

The basis of sociology is the understanding of the interactions of individuals with others in society and studying the institutions that contribute to their development. These institutions lead to their belief systems of right and wrong and their unique set of values. The institutions include family, school, church, and other organizations. In the case of both Fulks and Basham, it also includes the criminal justice and mental health systems, as will be noted in the paragraphs below. In the 1970s, Judge Bazelon suggested that sociological and psychological theories be considered in what he characterized as the *rotten social background* theory.

If the *rotten social background* theory ever had a place in the understanding the actions of individuals, it is with Fulks and Basham. In the law, these are often also called *mitigating factors*.

Mitigating factors do not justify or excuse an offense but may reduce the severity of a charge by contextualizing it. *Mitigating factors* include mental capacity and childhood background, childhood physical abuse, and childhood sexual abuse. In this case, the *mitigating factors* are included not to excuse their behavior but to explain it and try to understand what kind of individuals they were, and why they were not to be deterred by ordinary measures, and perhaps not even extraordinary measures, since they were willing to escape from jails, shoot it out with cops, pursue high speed chases, and attempt to run a police officer down.

Psychopathy

This is the official diagnostic definition of psychopathy at the time, issued in 1994, at the time of the event:

DSM-IV-TR Diagnostic Criteria for Antisocial Personality Disorder (301.7)

A. There is a pervasive pattern of disregard for and violation of the rights of others occurring since age 15 years, as indicated by three (or more) of the following:

1.   failure to conform to social norms with respect to lawful behaviors as indicated by repeatedly performing acts that are grounds for arrest
2.   deceitfulness, as indicated by repeated lying, use of aliases, or conning others for personal profit or pleasure
3.   impulsivity or failure to plan ahead
4.   irritability and aggressiveness, as indicated by repeated physical fights or assaults
5.   reckless disregard for safety of self or others
6.   consistent irresponsibility, as indicated by repeated failure to sustain consistent work behavior or honor financial obligations
7.   Lack of remorse, as indicated by being indifferent to or rationalizing having hurt, mistreated, or stolen from another.

B. The individual is at least age 18 years.

C. There is evidence of conduct disorder with onset before age 15 years.

D. The occurrence of antisocial behavior is not exclusively during the course of schizophrenia or a manic episode.

Sociopaths, psychopaths, and anti-social personal disorders are often used interchangeably, and the differences are largely academic and theoretical, not practical, differences. The checklist describes both Fulks and Basham. Being a psychopath means being a risk-taker and not caring about consequences. It is the psychopathy that makes them irrational actors, and that is what in turn makes these individuals so undeterrable. The check list of psychopathy advanced by Dr. Robert D. Hare was used.[60]

Dr. David B. Adams, a clinical psychologist[61], adds some additional nuances to the definition of psychopath based on his clinical experience, which again apply to both Fulks and Basham. The psychopath understands the wishes and concerns of others, but doesn't care. He rarely has a regular job. He repeatedly abuses, abandons, or betrays sexual partners, and any children he produces. Psychopaths are liars, they're evasive, they feign forgetfulness, and give vague and inconsistent answers about their past. They may lie for the fun of it.

Even when confessing, they may give flimsy excuses, and then go back to lying again. They are quick to anger. They don't know love, only sexual attraction or physical comfort or material support. What the psychopath calls sadness may be the failure of his most recent manipulative attempts. They rely upon alcohol and illicit drugs from very early in life. They have a fascination with fear. The pain they inflict upon their victims and society as a whole makes it difficult to imagine wanting to help them. Finally, true remorse does not exist in a psychopath, according to Dr. Adams.

The background information on Fulks and Basham is presented below to point out the characteristics that made them psychopaths, and, therefore, irrational actors. From most accounts, Fulks was the ringleader, but both fit the definitions of psychopaths and irrational actors, as can be seen from the material presented in the following paragraphs. At the time of the crime, Fulks was 25, and Basham was 21. That also places them squarely in the category of the most common crime-committing age cohort (18-25) and also the most common age for psychopathy. Clinically, psychopathy, sociopathy, and anti-social personality disorder are not diagnosed until age 18, and it is commonly agreed that psychopathy can be outgrown by the fourth or fifth decade—not soon enough to save Burns and Donovan.

Backgrounds of Perpetrators

The backgrounds of these perpetrators help one to understand why they were so vicious, ruthless, and therefore undeterrable. The Supreme Court (in Wiggins) has clearly said that a family history assessment is appropriate, and is virtually always necessary, when there are indications of a troubled family background. (Judge in Fulks 18-143).

The irrational actor theory is substantiated by the backgrounds of the two perpetrators creating the life experiences that led to their criminal lifestyles and the difficulty of deterring them through any reasonable measures. There is little doubt that they were psychopaths from the descriptions of their lifestyles, behavior, and diagnoses by psychiatrists at their trials. They had already escaped from jail together and were willing to escape from cops, including their attempts to kill cops, until they were finally captured.

The separate backgrounds of Fulks and Basham are taken up below under the following categories:

- Drugs
- Childhood Circumstances
- Childhood Violence
- Marital/Relationship Background
- Fulks in Charge/Basham as Follower
- Mental Condition
- Police, Guards, and Escapes
- Mitigating Circumstances
- Bonding

Fulks

Drugs

- Fulks says they were smoking crank at the time of the abduction of Burns (p. 6 WVSP). The use of drugs at the time of a crime supports the irrational actor theory.
- Fulks says that meth is the devil's drug and is the reason he is where he is today (on death row). He said it takes your ability to think away, and he was on meth, cocaine, weed, and drank daily." (p. 4. on 7/3/06 from Fulks' *Interviews with the Condemned*).
- According to Hopkins County, Kentucky Jail records, Fulks had a history of drug use, possession of drug paraphernalia and marijuana.
- Chad's brother, Dewayne Fulks, in the South Carolina trial, Vol. IV at page 105, said they all did meth together in November.
- U. S. Court of Appeals, p. 5, refers to trial testimony of Fulks' drug use that in November 8, 2002, he smoked marijuana and meth with his brother Ronnie. He later met a young woman named Heather Jacobi, with whom he used drugs.
- In statements to the FBI in 2003, Fulks said they smoked meth before driving to the Barboursville Mall, near Huntington (p. 5 of Appeal).
- On November 15, 2002, Fulks and Basham arrived in Huntington, WV and spent the next two nights smoking crack cocaine at Beth McGuffin's. (Appeal, p. 7)
- At SC Trial Vol VII, p. 261, Ronnie Fulks, Chad's brother, testifies that on Friday, November 8th, he, Dewayne, Chad, and Tina Severance did marijuana, meth, and drank alcohol. He agrees that with meth, you can stay awake for a long period of time. He met Basham and Andrea Roddy that night. At p. 262, "We was up for few days." November 19th (p. 263), Chad came back by himself, driving Donovan's BMW and asked for weed (p. 266). Chad said the other boy (Basham) got stupid. He and his girlfriend Andrea Beretta gave Chad a ride on the

20th of November, the day he was arrested.

- FBI p. 49, Fulks says he was smoking crank that night before the mall (November 11, 2002).
- FBI p. 175, Fulks said he had meds for nerves in jail but none since his escape.
- Veronica Evans, Chad's second wife, testified at SC trial, Vol XIII, from pp. 90-216 that she and Chad used alcohol and marijuana when they were together.
- Chad is drinking alcohol, smoking marijuana, and huffing gas on a regular basis, at age 14. (Andrews 18-170)

Childhood Circumstances

Arlene Andrews is the social worker for the defense who provided the family genogram (family history). (Vol 18, beginning at p. 125).

"His father, Roger, married his mother, Diana. You will see they were divorced before they had children, and then they had children starting with the sister Sherri, his brother Dwayne, his brother Ronnie, himself, his younger brother Shannon". (Andrew 18-137). They divorced because when Roger was in Viet Nam, his sister said Diana was having sex with another man and living with another man. When he returned they remarried.

"Probably the thing that was most unusual, and I have interviewed lots of families, was the amazingly poor recall that both of his parents had. I talked to Roger and Diana. They live separately in separate states now. They simply cannot remember Chad very well as a child. His father told me that he doesn't remember Chad at all until he was about 12, even though he lived in the house with him." (Andrews at 18-138). His mother does not remember when he was born. It was in a doctor's office, and there are no records.

By the time Chad was 12 or 13, he was following his older brother Dewayne everywhere, "except Dewayne was in prison." Chad was still in a class for behaviorally disordered children, in sixth grade, but his grades were getting worse. (Andrews 18-164).

He's involved with a handgun at 12 or 13, pointing it at an 11-year-old boy. (Andrews 18-165) A month before turning 14, he attempted suicide. (Andrews 18-167).

At age 14, he went to Indiana to live with his dad, had trouble at school, reading at the 4th grade level and the psychiatric evaluation at that time says he has a sociopathic pattern and a history of being molested by an older man. (Andrews 18-169)

[He had] exposure to the drinking, drugs, and fighting adult neighbors, or people hanging out at the house. Tolerance for children's alcohol and drug use. Periods when the parents didn't look for work. Chad really didn't have anyone who modeled for him how to live in a responsible, economically self-sufficient family life. He was taught to steal. There were these loose sexual boundaries with the mother's nudity. The parents were accusing each other of affairs. The parents accepted his relationship with an older woman when he was only 15. Many parents wouldn't stand for that. There was pornography, watching videos, magazines. (Andrews 18-183).

Fulks says growing up was hard for him, that "We kids would hide behind the couch when things were bad at home." He raised himself from 14 on, had speech problems, never had nice clothes, and the kids made fun of him. (p. 2 on 7/3/06 of Fulks' *Interviews with the Condemned*).

Dewayne Fulks, his brother, says that there was sometimes no food in the house, and he would steal food from convenience stores and neighbors' houses. When you turned on the lights, in the house, you had to wait for the bugs to leave (SC trial, Vol. 17, p. 121).

At SC Vol. 17, 122, Dewayne says that not one of the five (siblings) graduated from high school.

At Fulks' WV sentencing, at p. 52, his IQ is noted to be in the high 70s, which is borderline mentally retarded.

In the Appeal, p. 11, defense counsel had stated in trial that Fulks was a victim of Fetal Alcohol Spectrum Disorder and had been raised in abject poverty by alcoholic, abusive parents who neglected his education, encouraged criminality, and failed to provide him with the basic necessities of life.

In SC trial, vol. 17, Dr. Evans, a neuropsychologist, testifies, as an expert for the defense, regarding Fulks, (p. 5-28). Fulks' IQ was 75 to 79 with borderline intellectual functioning, reading at the 6th to 7th grade level. Tests suggested frontal lobe malfunctioning, as well as left temporal, finding he was moderately impaired, and he would have problems with executive functions. With this, you have a tendency to act impulsively, he testified, and not think about the consequences of your actions. You are likely to have bad judgment and bad decision-making. (Cross-examination p. 28-67) I don't think he was ever diagnosed as psychotic. Fulks had claimed the TV was talking to him in a 1998 evaluation. Brain damage puts individuals at high risk for behaviors such as rape. (8% are under 79 IQ). It's brain damage in conjunction with family, environmental, circumstantial, alcohol variables and upbringing that makes the difference. It can be exacerbated with alcohol or stress or other things you have ingested, Dr. Evans says.

Cindy Harper pp. 73-75 of SC trial, vol. 17, was a kindergarten teacher for Fulks. He was quiet, shy, and had difficulty learning, she said. One day he had a bad case of diarrhea and messed up his jeans and cowboy boots, and his parents never came and picked him up, so it was a very embarrassing situation.

Gayle Wolfe (pp 75-83 of SC trial vol. XVII) was his special education teacher. She taught Fulks in 5th grade. He was a slow learner, she said, but he tried hard, and he wanted to learn. He lived in a poor neighborhood. When she visited, his parents offered her a beer in the front yard.

Martha Floyd, SC trial pp. 84-94, vol, XVII, taught Chad in 6th grade, special education class. He was eager to please and lacked school supplies and clothes. One of the teachers bought him shoes. He wasn't disruptive, but she saw bruises on him.

Sue Hatcher, social worker (SC trial vol. XVII, pp. 95-109), said Fulks was assigned to her when she was a probation officer, and he was 9-years-old. At that time, he had already been charged with two batteries. One was of an elderly woman, and the second was of a four or five year old girl on the playground, whom he asked for money and pulled her pants down. His older brother Ronnie was also involved. At age 12, he held a gun to a child's head at a pizza restaurant. His parents were alcoholics. There were a lot of reports of him bullying in the school and neighborhood. The police officer for juveniles (p. 103, S. C. trial, Vol. XVII) thought he should be removed from the home, and that police officer, Allen Meek is now Chief of Police of Barboursville. He thought when Chad was nine that he ought to be removed from his home. Cross-Examination, SC trial, Vol. XVII, p. 105 indicates there is no evidence that Fulks was charged on the childhood offenses. This testimony was followed by Dr. Becker's testimony that Fulks suffers from Fetal Alcohol Syndrome (S. Carolina trial, Vol, XVII, beginning at p. 109).

In cross-examination (SC trial, Vol XIII, p. 10 and on), Ronnie Fulks testified that they did not have an easy childhood, their parents drank all day every day until they got staggering, passing out drunk, and their parents smoked marijuana.

Gayle Beatty, at SC Trial Vol 16, beginning on p. 147, Chad's aunt, testifies. Her sister is Chad's mother, Diana, and she states that she (the aunt) loves Chad. She remembers giving Chad money for candy when he was little, and instead, he bought her a pair of earrings (p. 156). Their grandmother didn't want Chad and his brothers at her house because she was afraid they would steal something. Chad asked his aunt Gayle if he could come home with her (to live). At p. 159, she says she wishes she could have taken him because she feels like the whole system failed him and that their family was ignored.

Mark Fulks, Chad's uncle, Chad's father's brother, in testimony at SC trail, Vol XVI, beginning at p.159, testifies that his brother and wife were alcoholics. At p. 169, the house was crowded and dirty, with cockroaches, and no food. He said the father refused to testify for Chad at this trial and wouldn't visit him in prison. At cross-examination, he said their mother left him with the kids when Chad was 14 and turned her life over to God.

He got his high school equivalency, GED; earned a certificate as a welder. (SC p. 192)

Childhood Violence

Dewayne Fulks, at the SC trial, Vol. IV, p. 122, Chad's brother, said their parents were usually drunk, and the police were constantly at their house (SC p. 119). He said that his dad heard the police calls on the scanner so often regarding calls to the little blue house on the corner that he painted the house yellow.

Dewayne Fulks (SC trial Vol. IV, p. 126) says that he taught Chad how to break into cars. At p. 122, he says that his dad hit all of them, and at p. 116, says that his parents physically fought. These are the three factors that support the coaching theory. Dewayne Fulks confirms all three for Chad, he saw violence when his parents fought, he experienced it, when he was hit by his dad and mother, and he was coached into it, by Dewayne. Dewayne said that it (the violence) affected Chad more. He was more emotional and cried a lot (SC trial, Vol IV, at p. 132).

In cross-examination (SC trial, Vol XIII, p. 10 and on), Ronnie Fulks, Chad's brother, also testified that his parents physically fought, and his mother would throw whatever she could find at his father--ketchup bottle, coffee pot, ashtrays. Their mother would beat them even more than their father would beat them (p. 14). Ronnie and his brothers fought in the neighborhood and would beat up new kids just because they were new (p. 15). Ronnie took the blame for one of his father's crimes of messing up someone's car, when he was 16, and left the state. Ronnie got in trouble for the first time at school when he was in kindergarten and beat up a sixth grader, but after that, everyone left him alone (p. 20). He's only 5'2", but his mother refused to give him growth hormones, He no longer speaks to her because she wouldn't let him parole to her house, and he had to remain incarcerated in an Ohio prison fourteen months longer for aggravated assault and burglary.

Gayle Beatty, at SC Trial Vol 16, beginning on p. 147, Chad's aunt, testifies that she saw Chad's father beat the boys.

Mark Fulks, Chad's uncle, Chad's father's (Roger) brother, in testimony at SC trail, Vol XVI, beginning at p.159, testifies that Chad's mother and father fought like two men fighting in a bar. Mark asked him why he stayed with her, and he said he wouldn't be able to get another woman because he had "no teeth at all" and the only way they could tolerate each other was by drinking. He said they drank a case and a half of beer a day. At p. 168, he testifies that he had seen the parents kick the kids and throw things at them. They'd hide under the car, and he would kick them while they were under there. Roger tattooed the kids when they were young. His parents would call them names like "cocksucking mother-fucker bastard".

By the time he was 15, Chad was back in WV in a group home for setting a fire and needing alcohol and drug counseling.

He's involved with a handgun at 12 or 13, pointing it at an 11 year old boy. (Andrews 18-165)

Marital/Relationship Background

At Fulks' SC criminal trial, Amber Fowler, his first wife, testified (pp 31-79, Vol XV). She began dating him when she was 16, and Chad was 16. When he was sent to a juvenile facility, she became pregnant with another man. That son, Devon, was born May 28, 1995, and Chad and Amber were married July 6th, 1995. They all three lived with Amber's mother. Devon died November 10, 1995. After they married, Chad started hitting her in the back of the head and face and would drag her through the house by her hair. They moved to Myrtle Beach, SC the last part of 1995.

He never worked when they were married. He made a living by stealing. I would watch to make sure nobody was coming when he broke windows out of cars and stole people's stuff. He would do this at malls, golf courses, miniature golf courses, and at the beach. He drank alcohol and smoked crack. When they moved back to Kenova, WV, they stayed at the Hollywood motel, and then he got arrested. (The Hollywood Motel is also where he stayed the night of the Samantha Burns' abduction.)

P. 2-3, US. Court of Appeals, Fulks, who grew up in the tri-state area around Huntington, WV, began dating an exotic dancer named Veronica Evans in April, 2002. He lived with her and her three year old son Miles and they were married on June 11, 2002 (discrepancy). "He supported his new family in the same way he had supported himself for years—by breaking into cars and stealing. And as he had with other women, Fulks often became violent with Evans, sometimes beating her severely and assaulting her sexually." On August 25, 2002, Evans reported to police that Fulks was in the parking lot with a gun and that she was afraid he would kill her.

Tina Severance testified at the SC Trial, beginning at p. 19 of Vol IV. She was a correctional officer at Westville Correctional

Institute in Westville, Indiana, and Chad Fulks was one of her inmates. She worked nights, and Fulks told her he had observed her having sex with another inmate. She developed a relationship with Fulks after the other inmate was released. She talked and wrote letters with Fulks, but says it was not physical while he was in jail. She weighed 280 pounds but after a gastric bypass later, she lost 100 pounds in four to six months. Fulks said he loved her. She was terminated in May, 2002. Fulks was released March 22, 2002, and he came to live with her and her daughter, and she says they had sex only once. He was on parole at that time. He began selling cologne and met a stripper named Veronica Evans within three weeks and moved in with her and married her instead of Tina.

Tina loved him, she said, because he was beautiful and being the size she was, she didn't think she had a lot of options and thought he would come back to her. He did, in fact, call her when Veronica stabbed him numerous times in the arm. Tina later received word that he was arrested in September 2002 and was at Hopkins County Detention Center in KY. After his escape from Hopkins, he showed up at her mobile home on November 6, 2002, where she lived with Andrea Roddy. Basham (under a false name) was with him, and Basham and Andrea had a sexual relationship. Tina was with Fulks throughout the crime spree, but Fulks and Basham left her and Andrea in South Carolina. They had no money to get back home until sometime later, when the FBI provided them a bus ticket and some money for other items and the hotel. Prior to that, Fulks threatened her with a gun at one point during the crime spree and said she wasn't going anywhere.

They had Samantha's ID but threw it away (p. 177). Fulks and Severance began corresponding after he was arrested for the murders. She still loves him even after learning about the murders. At p. 209, Vol III, SC trial, Fulks lies in a letter in 2001, when he was incarcerated at Westville, implying that he has a son Devon who is alive, but he never had a child of his own, and Devon died in 1995. From Hopkins, before he escaped, he wrote declaring his love for her and saying he is trying to get divorced from Veronica and asks her to marry him (p. 229), but he was already divorced. She responded that she would marry him. At p. 256, he talks about being upset by statements she made to the FBI. His letters from prison after the murders are filled with smiley faces and puppy dog eyes, in a continued attempt to manipulate her even from prison.

Veronica Evans, Chad's second wife, testified at SC trial, Vol XIII, from pp. 90-216. She's 24 and was raised in foster care. She dropped out of high school her senior year because she was pregnant and lived in a shelter because of her abusive boyfriend. After that, she became pregnant by another man. The attorney says at p. 101, "So, just to keep it straight. As far as your children, Darren was the father of Nevada, Delbert is the father of Miles, and then you had a third child with Dennis, is that correct? You are living with Dennis, you are giving Nevada up for adoption, and Miles is living with you and Dennis". Her own father physically and sexually abused her (at p. 102), as did her foster father. Both her father and that man are now dead. April 2002, she met Chad, while stripping at a club.

Veronica's aunt was a dancer there too. Veronica had never agreed to marry any of the three fathers of her three children, but she agreed to marry Chad, and they married on June 11, 2002 in Ashland, KY. But before that in May, 2002, she told Chad she wanted to move back to Dennis, and he punched her in the nose. After that, he continued to physically and sexually abuse her, having sex six to ten times a day. He was very sexually motivated, she says. Another time, he put a knife to her throat and said "This is what I [Veronica] get for toying with people's hearts". p. 121. Fulks didn't work, he got money by breaking into cars, she said, stealing purses or anything he could find in beach accesses or state parks at Myrtle Beach (p. 126). They were both arrested in August 2002. Another time, he hit her with a gun and burned her face with a cigarette (p. 129).

Later, he broke into a car and got FBI clothes, put them on, and with a badge, held up some kids, who thought he was FBI. At one point, she urinated in his mouth, at his request, and then against her will, he urinated in hers making her throw up (p. 138). He beat her up in Myrtle Beach, and she called the police (p. 141) but ends up back with him. He later handcuffs her, prods her with a bow and arrow and repeatedly rapes her. At p. 154, on August 26th, 2002, she called 911 from a Wal-Mart, and the police came and arrested both of them and placed them in the Hopkins County Jail. Living with him for five months was hell, she testifies at p. 162. In cross-examination, at p. 169, she is said to be bipolar, and she is questioned about her role in the violence. At p. 217, she says: "I did whatever Chad wanted me to. As long as I was good and I behaved, then I didn't get the shit knocked out of me." At p. 225, in redirect, not one charge has been brought against her for laying a finger on any of her children.

At 15, Chad was living as boyfriend/girlfriend with a woman in her late twenties. His childhood was essentially over, and he never lives at home again. (Andrews 18-171).

"Look at the forensics in this case and remember whose semen is on the back seat of Alice Donovan's car" [Fulks']. (Defense closing argument in Basham 29-155).

"Here is a man -- here is a man who has beaten and physically abused just about every woman in his life. Think about the testimony you heard from Amber Fowler, and Heather Goodman, and from Veronica Evans. Where he would punch them. Where he would slap them. Where he would kick them. Where he would blacken their eyes. Where he would bloody their nose. Where he would bloody their lips. Where he would make them suck on the end of a gun barrel. Where he would pistol-whip them. That is how he treated the women in his life." (Gasser in Fulks' closing 21-68)

Mental Condition

Dr. Bachman, at Fulks' trial, vol. 18 at p.14, neurologist. Finds low mental status and frontal lobe problems, indicating dementia and brain impairment and fetal alcohol syndrome (p. 18). There is evidence of brain dysfunction. "He has got an abnormal MRI scan. He has an abnormal pet scan. Quantitative analysis of the CAT scan was done. Neuropsychological testing was done on several different occasions". (Dr. Bachman 18-70). And they measured his general intellectual ability at 77-79 (Dr. Bachman, 18-77).

Dr. Ruben Gur at 12-31, a cognitive neuroscientist testifies that he has a highly abnormal brain (12-41). He has a cyst on his brain (12-78). And the brain is misshapen. Essentially a baby with fetal alcohol syndrome is born drunk and has to spend the first few months going through withdrawal. (12-91). "I haven't seen a brain quite as abnormal as that of Mr. Fulks". (12-147).

You can't fake an MRI or PET. What affects him is judgment, impulse control, long term goals and acting in accordance with what is good for you and decision making. (Gur, 12-138). "I'm not saying he is retarded, he is clearly not a very bright individual. He is less intelligent than the average person." IQ is in high 70s. (Gur 12-140).

Dr. Andrew Simcox is a Ph.D. in forensic psychology. He and his team of other psychologists and social workers spent 43 days evaluating Mr. Fulks' conduct, and evaluating tests and MRI's in 1998 at a Federal medical facility in Kentucky. Fulks was charged with interstate transportation of a stolen motor vehicle. (Attorney, 12-187 at side bar) In 1998, Fulks was diagnosed as having antisocial personality disorder and malingering. (12-102). No malingering in 2003 testing reported. (12-131). Malingering is intentional production of false or grossly exaggerated physical or psychological symptoms motivated by obvious external incentives. (Attorney from DSM 12-195).

"Anti-social Personality Disorder is a cluster of abhorrent personality traits characterized by pervasive pattern of disregard for and violation of the rights of others. This pattern begins in early adolescence and continues into adulthood and is characterized by deception, impulsive and irresponsible behavior, aggression, and lack of remorse." (Prosecuting Attorney from DSM-IV 12-196). The psychological team in 1998 clearly diagnosed Mr. Fulks as having an anti-social personality disorder. (Prosecuting Attorney 12-197). Defense expert Dr. Gur agrees that it is probably an axis to an appropriate diagnosis. (Gur 12-197). The essence of your testimony is that, his ability to make good decisions, correct decisions, appropriate decisions is impaired by his neurological dysfunction and most important, control of impulses." (Prosecuting Attorney 12-207 regarding Dr. Gur's testimony).

"The government has not only provided you a window into the dark and malicious heart of Chad Fulks, we have, literally, provided you a front row seat." And he will describe the "17 days of carnage that left two women dead and families destroyed." (Mr. Gasser in Closing 20-20 & 23).

"You have already heard from James Hawkins, the one live witness I told you about who gave you a display and told you about what Chad Fulks' demeanor was like, his intensity, his violence. Now you hear from Tina Severance, another live witness. The closest Tina Severance came to dying during that trip was when Chad Fulks had that gun pointed a foot from her head. He came within a squeeze of that trigger from putting a bullet into the head of Tina Severance, the woman that he loved".(Gasser in Closing at 20-55).

Blume, Defense for Fulks Closing Vol XXI, at p. 137. "You have heard Chad's confession. And, in it, he admitted that he raped Ms. Donovan; he admitted to being involved in the kidnapping and carjacking; he denied he killed either victim. He denied he knew, at that time, that Mr. Basham was going to kill either victim."

"But, you know, his parents do not care. And now, you know, at this moment, his parents don't care. And they are not here. But I do think we can safely say this. If Chad Fulks had been removed from the home when Sue Hatcher's probation officer made the recommendation, along with the police officer and principal, then we wouldn't be here today. If he had gone to live with his Aunt Gayle, we wouldn't be here today. If he had had parents who were even the least bit supportive, loving, who cared maybe even just a little, we wouldn't be here today in this courtroom." (Mr. Blume- Fulks' Defense Attorney Closing 21-170).

"The police officer, Allen Meek, thought he had to be removed. Police officer, Allen Meek, would not have been a bleeding heart. He becomes a police chief." (Johnson, Closing Fulks' Defense Attorney 21-199).

Fulks in Charge

"Brandon Basham was a puppet, and Chad Fulks was pulling his strings throughout a lot of this crime spree." (Gasser in closing 20-67).

Hawkins (at p. 4. of US Appeals) had testified at trial that

Basham merely followed Fulks' order. Fulks told Severance that he escaped because he feared a lengthy prison sentence on the pending child abuse charges.

November 14, 2002, at 2 PM, when Fulks and Basham burglarized his son's residence outside Conway, SC, Jordan said both Fulks and Basham fired gunshots at him. (p. 7 of Appeal).

McGuffin testified at trial that during the time she spent with Fulks and Basham, Fulks controlled what he and Basham did. (p. 8 of Appeal).

The prosecution at trial (Appeal, p. 10) stated that the crime spree touched on places with which Fulks, not Basham, was familiar, that shortly after their prison escape, Fulks had asked Severance where they could obtain guns, that Fulks had tied Hawkins to the tree, and both had fired at Jordan during the burglary.

Basham threatened Severance (after Burns) by asking her whether she wanted to go "swimming" in the Ohio River, which she took to mean drowning her. Fulks ordered him to stop, and Basham complied. (Appeal, p. 6). Tina Severance testified at SC trial, Vol III, p. 123, that after November 11th, Brandon kept singing a song by Shania Twain about how he was going to get me one way or the other, and he kept asking me if I wanted to go swimming (in the Ohio River). Chad told him to shut up, and he shut up.

In his letters, after the murders, Fulks continues to claim that Basham was to blame (Severance in Vol III, SC, p. 268).

According to Severance, Fulks kept her ID in his possession. (FBI p. 5).

Defense lawyer for Basham, arguing that Fulks was the leader:

"Who was the leader and who was the follower. Who was the puppeteer and who was the puppet. Ladies and Gentlemen, Chad Fulks is an evil person. Chad Fulks is a con man. Chad Fulks has a history of doing that to other people, and he had a history, in this case, of doing worse than despicable acts." (Defense closing in Basham 29-157).

Prosecution lawyer in Basham, arguing that there was no leader:

"You recall the best explanation for Chad Fulks and Brandon

Basham during that time period. Tina Severance said, like two peas in a pod." (Prosecutor's closing in Basham 29-270).

Police, Guards & Escapes

"We are going to show photographs where his client (Fulks) took a chunk out of the flesh of a security guard for future dangerousness." (Attorney in Colloquy 12-220).

"And he [Fulks] goes on a high-speed chase, 128 miles an hour, with no lights on, zigging in and out of traffic, crossing the median. The defense would have you believe that he wasn't a threat, that this was not a violent act, that he wasn't a threat to the people on that highway. Ladies and Gentlemen, he threatened the lives of trooper Hunter. He almost killed trooper Malo. (Gasser at Fulks' Closing 21-90).

Mitigating Circumstances

In the SC trial, vol. 22, pp 30-35, each mitigating circumstance that was presented at trial was voted upon by the jury. That finding is presented below for Fulks with the number of the twelve jurors who voted in consideration of the factor in bold. If they did not vote for it, it does not mean that they did not agree that the factor existed, but rather that it should not be considered as a mitigating circumstance in his guilt or innocence.

Mitigating Factors Fulks SC Trial, Vol XXII p. 30-35

- Chadrick Evan Fulks's mother abused alcohol while she was pregnant with him. **12.**
- Chadrick Evan Fulks's brain was permanently damaged by his mother's drinking during her pregnancy. **9.**
- Chadrick Evan Fulks has an IQ between 77 and 79. **4.**
- Chadrick Evan Fulks's ability to process information is impaired because he has fetal alcohol spectrum disorder. **0.**
- Chadrick Evan Fulks's ability to control his impulses is impaired because he has fetal alcohol spectrum disorder. **1.**

- Chadrick Evan Fulks's ability to make good decisions is impaired because he has fetal alcohol spectrum disorder. **0.**
- Chadrick Evan Fulks's ability to understand cause-and-effect and predict the consequences of his actions is impaired because he has fetal alcohol spectrum disorder. **0.**
- Chadrick Evan Fulks's ability to learn from his mistakes is impaired as a result of neurological damage. **0.**
- Chadrick Evan Fulks suffered from learning disabilities as a child. **12.**
- Chadrick Evan Fulks tried hard in school but could never do well. **0.**
- Chadrick Evan Fulks's parents cared so little for his education that they never helped him with homework and even left him at school with soiled pants. **10.**
- Chadrick Evan Fulks was neglected by both of his parents. **12.**
- Chadrick Evan Fulks lived in a house that was often filthy and infested with roaches and rats. **12.**
- Chadrick Evan Fulks's parents did not provide him with adequate clothing or school supplies. **12.**
- Chadrick Evan Fulks frequently went hungry or was uncertain whether he would get food as a child. **11.**
- Chadrick Evan Fulks's parents sold food stamps to get money for beer. **12.**
- Chadrick Evan Fulks's parents drank to excess almost every day. **6.**
- Chadrick Evan Fulks was often left without supervision. **12.**
- Chadrick Evan Fulks was permitted to roam the streets as a young child. **12.**
- A principal, a police officer, and a probation officer all recommended Chadrick Evan Fulks be removed from the home at the age of 9, but he was not removed. **12.**
- Chadrick Evan Fulks's parents gave him little attention or affection. **12.**
- Chadrick Evan Fulks was subjected to emotional abuse

as a child. **12.**

- Chadrick Evan Fulks was subjected to physical abuse as a child. **12.**
- Chadrick Evan Fulks grew up seeing his parents frequently fighting each other. **12.**
- Chadrick Evan Fulks grew up seeing heavy drinking and frequent fighting by other adults in his own house. **12.**
- Chadrick Evan Fulks learned at home that violence and fighting were a normal part of relationships between men and women. **4.**
- Chadrick Evan Fulks grew up seeing pornographic photographs of naked women papering the walls and ceiling of his basement. **12.**
- Chadrick Evan Fulks's father showed him pornographic movies as a young child. **12.**
- Chadrick Evan Fulks's mother was often half-dressed around the house. **0.**
- Chadrick Evan Fulks was sexually abused as a child. **0.**
- Chadrick Evan Fulks started drinking at age nine and using marijuana at 11 or 12, and his parents made no effort to stop him. **12.**
- Chadrick Evan Fulks's brother taught him to inhale gasoline and paint as a young teenager. **12.**
- Chadrick Evan Fulks's father encouraged him to steal. **0.**
- Chadrick Evan Fulks's mother ignored his stealing. **12.**
- Chadrick Evan Fulks's brothers taught him to steal, fight, and break into cars. 12.
- Chadrick Evan Fulks attempted suicide at age 13. **12.**
- Chadrick Evan Fulks was diagnosed with depression, substance abuse, and possible sociopathic tendencies at age 14. **10.**
- Chadrick Evan Fulks's capacity to conform his conduct to the requirements of law was impaired. **0.**
- Chadrick Evan Fulks took part in the offenses under mental and/or emotion disturbance. **0.**
- Chadrick Evan Fulks was under the influence of

alcohol and drugs at the time of his offenses. **0.**
- Other factors in Chadrick Evan Fulks's childhood, background, or character weigh against imposition of a sentence of death. **1.**
- No one has escaped from a high-security federal prison since 1993. **8.**
- Chadrick Evan Fulks pleaded guilty to kidnapping and carjacking, resulting in death. **12.**

We, the jury, as to Chadrick Evan Fulks, unanimously find, beyond a reasonable doubt, that the aggravating factors proved in this case outweighs the mitigating factors so as to justify a sentence of death; or in the absence of any mitigating factor, that the aggravating factor or factors alone justify a sentence of death. We, therefore, unanimously conclude that Chadrick Evan Fulks shall be sentenced to death. Signed by all jurors and the foreperson, Richard Gohrig, on June 30th, 2004.

From the mitigating factors above, all 12 jurors agreed that the ones below were mitigating factors for Fulks based upon the evidence produced at trial.

- His mother abused alcohol while she was pregnant with him.
- He suffered from learning disabilities.
- He was neglected by both of his parents.
- He lived in a house infested with roaches and rats.
- His parents did not provide him with adequate clothing or school supplies.
- His parents sold food stamps to get money for beer.
- He was often left without supervision.
- He was permitted to roam the streets as a young child.
- A principal, a police officer, and a probation officer all recommended he be removed from the home at the age of 9, but he was not removed.
- His parents gave him little attention or affection.
- He was subjected to emotional abuse as a child.

- He was subjected to physical abuse as a child.
- He grew up seeing his parents frequently fighting each other.
- He grew up seeing heavy drinking and frequent fighting by other adults in his own house.
- He grew up seeing pornographic photographs of naked women papering the walls and ceiling of his basement.
- His father showed him pornographic movies as a young child.
- He started drinking at age nine and using marijuana at 11 or 12, and his parents made no effort to stop him.
- His brother taught him to inhale gasoline and paint as a young teenager.
- His mother ignored his stealing.
- His brothers taught him to steal, fight, and break into cars.
- He attempted suicide at age 13.

Basham

Drugs

- Mrs. Basham said she used marijuana when she was pregnant with Basham, and they smoked crack cocaine together even recently (25-76 of Basham SC trial) At SC 26-123, Dr. Watts said Mrs. Basham told her that she used drugs during the pregnancy and admitted to marijuana use. Her son Tommy told her his mother used PCP, cocaine, and speed as well (p. 32-123).
- His sister told Dr. Brawley that she smoked marijuana with Brandon, and he would steal it from his mother who grew it. (SC 25-77). Charlotte also said he started huffing gas at age 8 and smoking crack cocaine at age 12, when he was living with his father. His mother and sister said it escalated over the years. The people Brawley interviewed all confirmed Basham's drug use from a young age to the present (SC 25-79). Huffing destroys brain cells (Dr. Watts, 26-255 SC).
- At p. 43 of the WV sentencing hearing, his attorney said that Basham was given illegal drugs when he was still on the

bottle, that he was given drugs and physically and sexually abused, and "I've never seen a record of abuse and neglect (like this) in 20 years (of practice)".

- At 77, of SC trial, Vol IV, Roddy says Chad and Brandon were smoking marijuana.
- The Ashland KY Police investigation reports that Basham shot at police (at p. 58), and he said he had cocaine at noon and marijuana at 2 PM, shortly before the attempted abduction in Ashland, KY.
- Basham says in SC after Donovan that he got high on the way back to Myrtle Beach (FBI p. 205).
- FBI at p. 128, Severance says they all got drunk and smoked marijuana on 11/12/02 in SC. FBI p. 124, Severance says that on November 9, 2002, they all smoked marijuana and drank alcohol.
- "The drug use is noted throughout his records", according to Dr. Brawley, the neuropsychologist at SC 25-168.
- "Mr. Basham has substance dependence for cocaine, marijuana, and inhalants." (Dr. Watts, SC 27-12).
- "And then, thirdly, some of his noncompliance, he trades his medicines for money, and food, and commissary. Sometimes that medication has been used to barter for needs." (Watts, 27-35).
- Dr. Capehart says he was dependent on cocaine, inhalants, and marijuana (27-182).
- "Brandon's mother drank and did drugs during her pregnancy. She would hold him when he was two years old and smoke a joint while she was nursing him. She would blow marijuana smoke into his face when he was two years old to try and calm him down. She would do drugs with Brandon. She would have him roll joints for her and her friends when he was still six and under." (Vogelsang, 20-41-42).

Childhood Circumstances

- According to Basham's sentencing hearing in WV, at p. 3, he reportedly had a 6th grade education.
- Vol 26, p. 166 of Basham SC Trial, he went through the 9th

grade.
- He is on social security and has never worked. (Attorney in SC trial 26-29).
- "I don't have any history that he has ever been gainfully employed. I know he has been on disability or social security since the age of ten." (Watts at SC 26-122).
- Brandon's mother has kidney failure and emphysema at the time of the trial. (Watts SC 26-109).
- "In my opinion, it is one of the worst developmental histories I have seen." "He has a mentally ill mother, he has surgery, he has minor head injuries, he has attention deficit disorder, he is using drugs." (Watts, SC 26-151).
- "Brandon's father has tried to slit his own throat. He dove out of a trailer onto his head trying to kill himself." (Vogelsang 20-34).
- "In looking at his history, it is clear that Brandon was born to parents whose histories were characterized by family violence, by substance abuse, by mental and emotional abuse, and behavioral impairments that had an impact on all of them, and by learning difficulties. Brandon was a special-needs child. He had head injuries as a child. He was physically abused. And he was in emotional behavioral disorder classes most of his school life. He was in special education most of his school life. But he was living in a home where he was completely corrupted and *missocialized*.
- He was taught all of the wrong things, all of the things you wouldn't want any child to learn, much less a special-needs child. Because of this, he missed out on the most important developmental stages. And what he did in response to this environment in his home is he developed something we call protective survival strategies, things such as drug use, lying, manipulation, aggression, and running away. In other words, he developed all of the wrong kinds of responses and reactions as a result of there not being anyone to get him through the developmental stages where he can learn the right things. And many other things that were similar to the ones I just mentioned.
- There was not anyone in his home that had any skills or any capacity to help him through developmental stages, to help

him master those stages, to offer him the support or the help that he needed. This is especially damaging with a childlike Brandon because he was a special-needs child. And while we may not be able to say definitively whether it was early drug use, or head injuries, or a combination of any of those things, it is clear that he was a special-needs child. Finally, the agencies and institutions that we count on to intervene on behalf of a child like Brandon, to act in their behalf and protect them, never did so in any kind of consistent way, any kind of long-term way, or any kind of way that was effective or helpful to him." (Vogelsang 20-35-37).

- "His behavior reflected violence, aggression, chaos, a lack of consistency, no understanding of consequences, no understanding of choices or responsibilities. It reflected the illegal behaviors that he saw in his home and was taught to engage in." (Vogelsang, p. 20-38).

- "His mother's way of waking Brandon up to go to school was to hit him." (20-60). She would steal dogs and cats from the neighbors and sell them for drugs. (20-59). As far as his mother's marriage to Brandon's father, Jimmy, she said "'it was either Jimmy or suicide, and she chose Jimmy." (Vogelsang 20-46).

- "Brandon's father also grew up in an environment that said it is okay to have sex with your sister, that is common behavior, that is not a problem. So, he (Brandon) kind of grew up in a sexual environment where things that we would consider inappropriate were not considered inappropriate by his family." (20-46).

- "He remained in school until around the 7th grade." (Vogelsang 20-82)

- He repeated first grade, and his parents were split up at that time. (SC trial 26-135, Watts).

- Suzanne Mayes said that Brandon was a management problem in school. No question he was developmentally and socially behind. (Defense closing argument, 29-136).

Childhood Violence

- His parents told Dr. Brawley that Brandon had a head injury when he was five or when he fell from a tree and hit his head on a metal railroad track. (SC 25-76). His parents said he was beat up frequently by other kids. He was small for his age, shunned because he was hyper, and he was depressed. His sister Charlotte told Dr. Brawley that Basham had been dropped on his head twice as an infant and was frequently beaten by his mother. (SC 25-77).

- From Hopkins County Jail Records, on 12/18/00, his psychiatrist, Dr. Seuss says that Basham is hallucinating about a man who sexually abused him as a child. [Sexual identity and childhood sexual abuse are characteristics of the indiscriminate felony murder classification, discussed previously.]

- Basham was released from a youth facility on his 18th birthday, in 1999 and is picked up on charges 56 days later. He is released again in May 2000. 61 days later, he is rearrested and placed in the Hopkins County Detention Center. He goes to Western State Hospital and is released on January 23, 2001, and he is picked up 13 days later when he is arrested and goes to Hopkins again until he escapes in November 2002.

- Mrs. Basham said she whipped him with a coat hanger when he was five (26-132 in SC trial testimony of Dr. Watts). [He experienced abuse].

- "The source reports Brandon was whipped by his mother with a coat hanger on his legs and buttocks." (Dr. Watts, 26-133 SC).

- He saw his sister Charlotte abused by her mother. She hit Charlotte's head against a brick wall (SC 26-134, Watts), and his parents fought. (Watts 26-136). [He saw abuse].

- "When Mr. Brandon Basham was a smaller child, he attempted to get in between them [his parents in a fight], and he was kicked in the stomach by Mr. Basham during that altercation." (Watts at SC trail 26-143).

- "Mr. Basham was latency age, meaning like from ages 8 to 12, when you are in elementary school years, that he reported that there was a homeless man that was taken in by his father. Basham reported that he was sodomized by this man." (Watts at SC 26-144).

- "There is documentation of Brandon and his sister both being abused as children. There were multiple reports made to their social services department. There were multiple visits by social services to their home, and some of the cases were opened or substantiated." (Vogelsang, 20-62).
- "The records indicate that they investigated the family from the time he was fifteen months old until the time he was fifteen years old." (20-67, Vogelsang).
- "But one of the worst things he witnessed was when his aunt shot his father in the leg. It was around Thanksgiving, he was about four years old. His father responded by, as I said earlier, grabbing her by the jaw at her mouth, dragging her, pulling the flesh. It was a very, very bloody battle scene for that family. And certainly stands out in the minds of all of the family members involved." (Vogelsang, p.20-70)
- "There is a cousin in the family who was, maybe, a 15-year-old young man, and someone that Brandon liked very much. And they were already, I believe, in high school, maybe in the 10th. And this was in Madisonville. And this young man liked a girl that another boy in the school liked. The other boy was very popular, had a lot of friends. And so these two sort of started fighting with each other over this girl--verbal arguments. And so, Brad would go home and complain to his dad, Larry, who is a family member on Brandon's father's side of the family. And Larry, being a loud, aggressive male in the family who drank and used drugs, said, "I will teach you on how to be a man.""
- So, he gets his son to agree to meet this young man and all of his friends at a cemetery in Madisonville at a graveyard. He puts his son Brad in the truck. He drives him over there. He says, "You will go confront all of these boys." And they got to the cemetery. Larry saw that the boy had brought six or seven other boys with him. He still forced Brad to get out of the car and go confront all of these young teenagers. And they picked Brad up by his feet, and they swung him against the grave stones and beat him until he died. And this is a story that is well-known in Madisonville." (Vogelsang, 20-70-72). [Coaching in violence].
- "The messages he got about how he handled problems and

conflicts were always to be aggressive or to cuss somebody out." (Vogelsang 20-73). [Coaching in violence].

- "But when Brandon was around 7 years old, his mother was dating Cliff Emerson, and she would stay at his apartment, which was a garage apartment in Madisonville, and she decided that she was going to break up with this guy. He had not long been released from prison, and she took Charlotte and Brandon with her to the garage apartment to confront him and to get her things. Charlotte was around 12 years old; Brandon was around seven. They went upstairs, and Cliff Emerson pulled a knife on Kathy, held it to her throat, and Kathy yelled for the children to run. She broke free of Cliff Emerson, and they all went running down the stairs, and Cliff Emerson came after Kathy. When they got downstairs into the garage, he got her on the ground again and was holding the knife to her throat, and Brandon jumped on top of him, and started beating him with his fist, and managed to get him to pull off of Kathy. And then he and Charlotte took off running, and Kathy took off running." (Vogelsang 20-72).

- "As he became older, he became more aggressive. He fought, he threatened others, he was very difficult to control in the classroom. By the time he got to group homes and psychiatric settings, he had to be restrained." (Vogelsang 20-83).

- "What finally put Brandon into Hopkins county jail for five years, was stealing social security money by writing bad checks off of his father's account." (Vogelsang 20-121)

Marital/Relationship Background

- At SC p 25-133, prior testing when he was 17 years old had shown that for Basham women were seen as objects of sexual gratification, and there was no indication of emotional or relational involvement.

- He has targeted female employees at correctional centers for masturbation episodes. (SC 25-134).

- "You heard from Dr. Watts that his attachment to women he just meets is almost pathological. That is Dr. Watts's testimony."(Prosecution closing in Basham 29-167).

- "At seven years of age, Brandon's sole desire when he grew up was to be a stripper. At seven years of age, he wanted to be a male stripper because at night, when his dad would get together with his friends, they would get him to stand on the table to perform." (Defense closing argument, 29-136).
- From Hopkins County, Kentucky jail records, "Basham was acting like a queer. On 12/17/01, he was trying to hug and kiss inmates." A letter in jail says "I'm having flashbacks of when I was abused."

Mental Condition

- He was diagnosed with Attention Deficit Disorder at age 7. (26-134 Watts, SC trial).
- At p. 409 of the WVSP, Kathy Basham says her son has ADD. According to Basham Death Row Speaks interview, his mother died July 2005.
- At 429, of WVSP, the judge ordered a psychiatric evaluation of Basham after his arrest, after the murders.
- His psychiatrist at Hopkins (Dr. Seuss) reports that Basham has mental problems and tried suicide twice in one day by hanging and by sticking his fingers in an electrical socket. Seuss reports that he was given valium for anxiety, and reports hallucinations, and has ADHD. He appears above average intelligence but has mood disorder and is bipolar. He is impulsive and inattentive, according to Dr. Seuss.
- According to McGuffin, at p. 414 of WVSP, Basham was really hyper and nervous.
- On 10/30/01, Basham's KY jail records indicate that the inmate had continuing medical issues. Basham tells you every symptom he has and more, Dr. Brawley testified, as a way of seeking attention (SC 25-149).
- In the SC trial, Vol IV, at p. 10, Tina Severance says that Basham was prepared to kill a police officer.
- At p. 55 of SC, Vol IV, Andrea Roddy says that Basham said if he had to shoot cops he would.
- At 112, of SC, Vol IV, Dewayne Fulks said Basham had a gun and said he wasn't "going out like that."

- FBI at p. 180, Fulks says Basham drove, but all other information indicated Fulks did all the driving. Fulks says Basham could drive but only automatic (FBI p. 52). FBI p. 5, Severance has never seen Basham drive and believes he does not know how. Roddy (FBI p. 19) said that Basham said he couldn't drive. His sister says he does not drive and never took the test (SC 21-82).

- Andrea Roddy says Basham used a fake name. (FBI, p. 17).

- Dr. Tora Brawley, Basham SC trial Vol XXV beginning at p. 18, forensic neuropsychologist testifies. Basham's IQ at SC trial pp. 25-38 and p, 53 defined by Dr. Brawley and his brain damage described at p. 51.

- Most of us are going to fall right there in the middle in the average range, that is from 90 to 109. About 50 percent of the population, as you can see from the 25th to the 74th percentile, falls in the average range. If you have a 130 or greater, you are very superior, you are in the top two percent of the population. If you are 69 or below, then you are in the extremely low or mentally retarded range in the bottom one to two percent of the population. He had a full-scale IQ of 68; a verbal IQ of 75; and, a performance IQ of 65.

- You are going to have decreases in attention concentration, memory problems, problems with judgment or reasoning, have problems -- solving problems, problems mental -- with mental tracking, insight, processing speed, and then, you oftentimes will see an increase in distractibility, apathy, irritability, depression, and any pre-existing personality traits.

- Dr. Brawley and Dr. Gourley (the prosecution doctor) both placed him in the mid to low borderline IQ. Dr. Gourley placed him at 75, and Dr. Brawley placed him at 68 (SC trial at 25-144). Dr. Brawley (at 25-56) says "Basham is the most distractible patient she ever had in 17 years. He had some real brain problems." (At 25-58). She did testing, interviewed him, interviewed family and friends, obtained school records and other records from institutions. Basham was diagnosed at 8 with ADHD. By age 10, he already had a history of huffing solvents. Records said he was grieving over his parents' divorce (25-63). He was treated with meds. At 35-66, records show at age 17, he was being harassed and bullied, leading to low self-esteem and was considered a high risk for suicide. Wendy Watts at the Hopkins County Schools told her Basham "didn't have a chance." (p. 25-70). His special-education teacher from 6th to 8th grade told her Basham had "big problems with concentration".

- He would live moment to moment. (25-73). He was very impulsive and his meds made a big difference. She thought he functioned at 4th grade level when he was in the 8th grade. At Hopkins County Detention Center, he scored at third-grade level (25-74). Also at Hopkins, Mr. Schaffer told her Basham was immature and did things that were not thought out. Anything would set him off. He was not flexible and not able to plan (25-75). She diagnosed him with dementia (cognitive deficits) due to multiple etiologies (causes). (SC 25-81 & 85). The causes of the brain damage were multiple head injuries, which have a cumulative effect, drug abuse of inhalants, marijuana, crack cocaine (SC 25-88). Learning disabilities and socioeconomic status make it worse and a lack of support system"

- Dr. Brawley doesn't think he is going to improve (25-92). Cross SC at pp. 25-100, he has a history of lying. He has difficulty benefiting from the consequences of his behavior as a result of his tendency to blame others for his problems. (SC 25-106). Attorney notes that he has the same disrespect for authority today that he had as a child (SC 25-109). And the attorney says his IQ was higher when he was younger and that his neurological exam was normal.

- "That is documented in the record that his IQ had been dropping over a number of years. And you heard testimony, as a result of the huffing that he had been doing." (Defense closing argument Basham 29-142).

- An MMPI in 1997 on Basham indicated the following, beginning at 25-140.

- "Adolescents with his profile are immature, impulsive, hedonistic, and frequently rebel against authority figures." He may be hostile, aggressive, and frustrated. He seems unable to learn from punishing, experiences, and repeatedly gets into the same type of trouble. Brandon has little ability to empathize with others and shows little or no remorse for his misbehaviors. He may be assaultive or very aggressive as he reports considerable problems in controlling his anger. Brandon may appear charming, intent to make a good first impression; however, his interpersonal relationships are likely to be very shallow. He is interested only in his own pleasure and is insensitive to the needs of others. He seems unable to experience guilt while causing others troubles."

- When Basham was a small child, Kathy Basham was hospitalized for a suicide attempt by overdosing on drugs (SC 26-130, Watts).

- Dr. Watts diagnoses him with dementia due to multiple etiologies (causes) caused by inhalant abuse, head injuries (Watts SC 26-251). Technically, it would be called substance induced persisting dementia and dementia secondary to head trauma. Watts, SC 26-252). Mr. Basham has an inability to learn new information or recall information.

- "The number of people that have noticed some kind of memory impairment over time--Brenda Thompkins, when he was eight years old; Dr. Rivard when he was 14; nurse Altman at the Pennyroyal Mental Health Center, D. Walker at Rice Audubon, Dr. Lunsford at Western State Hospital, Dr. Seuss, Dr. Brawley, Dr. Brannon, Dr. Gourley, Dr. Morgan, myself, and even Dr. Capehart in his evaluation, in his mental status examination of Mr. Basham, notes memory impairment". (Watts, SC 26-254).

- He has an impairment in judgment. (Watts, SC 26-254).

- He cannot plan ahead. "When he is focused on a concept, such as nicotine, that is all he is thinking about." (Watts, p. 26-262 SC).

- Some parts of his brain work, Dr. Watts testifies that Dr. Brawley found that (Watts, 26-266).

- Dr. Watts also diagnosed him with inhalant-induced psychosis, which accounts for hallucinations and hearing voices, Dr. Seuss saw similar behavior. (SC 26-266). When he is not on Concerta (for ADD) this is much more prevalent. (Watts, SC 26-270). She diagnoses him with and it is also clearly recorded that he has panic symptoms. So, he definitely has overwhelming anxiety. And we know that one of the triggers for that is him feeling boxed-in,

175

claustrophobic, not having his (cell) flap opened. (Watts, SC 26-272). He has bruised himself to keep from having his cell flap closed. (Watts, 26-272 SC). He has a history of hives, breaks out and itches. (SC 26-273).

- Watts diagnoses him with ADHD. (SC 27-5).
  - "I would have to say he is one of the most hyperactive individuals I have ever seen in my 11 years of practicing forensic psychiatry." (Dr. Watts, SC 27-8).
  - "And it basically consists of two different sets of symptoms. There are sets of symptoms that have to do with inattentiveness, that is the ability to pay attention to things. And you have to have these symptoms, a number of these symptoms, six of them. And you usually have to have onset of this disorder by the age of seven".
  - And Mr. Basham, clearly, if you go through the criteria out of section one, he meets the criteria for (a), often fails to give close attention to details, or makes mistakes in schoolwork, or other activities. He has criteria (b), he has a difficulty sustaining attention in tasks. Criteria (c), often does not seem to listen when spoken to directly. He has criteria (d), he does not follow through on instructions and fails to finish schoolwork, chores, or duties. He has criteria (e), difficulty organizing tasks and activities. Has criteria (f), he avoids and dislikes to engage in tasks that require sustained mental effort. He has definitely, probably to me, one of his most prominent symptoms is the criteria (h). That is, he is very easily distracted." (Watts, SC 27-6).
  - "This is the second part (of ADHD). We have inattentiveness and then the hyperactivity that goes with it. He has criteria (a), often fidgeting with hands, or feet, or squirms in seat. I have seen this during my testimony. I periodically check on Mr. Basham to see what he is doing. This has clearly been documented in his history. He would leave his seat in the classroom or in other situations where you are supposed to stay seated. Probably, the best doctor

that is in criteria (c) is Dr. Walker. He stated during his interview he walks about, climbs excessively in situations in which it is inappropriate. I think his description of Mr. Basham in his office running around, grabbing gloves, and the ear otoscope at the age of 16 clearly shows that. He has difficulty engaging in leisure activities quietly.

There are plenty of notes that talk about Mr. Basham making noises with his mouth, and that sort of thing. So, clearly, he meets that criterion. I think the most prominent symptom in this criteria is (e). He is often on the go or acts as if he is driven by a motor. I think that is his very hyper, high-speed activity, and that has been clearly noted. Like Dr. Cardona at the Stoner Creek Hospital, several people saw that high energy. It might be described as a mood disorder. I thought that was also consistent with attention deficit disorder. And often talks excessively, he also has that criteria. Under that, you have impulsivity that goes with attention deficit disorder. He meets requirement (h) [very easily distracted, and] (i) he has difficulty waiting for his turn, and he often interrupts or intrudes on others. (Watts, sc 27-8.)

- Dr. Watts diagnosed Basham with antisocial disorder [psychopathy, sociopathy], and also brain damage, with the symptoms and criteria listed below for antisocial disorder. (Watts, SC 27-14).
  - Criteria 1 "a failure to conform to social norms with respect to lawful behaviors as indicated by repeatedly performing acts that are grounds for arrest." (Watts 27-15).
  - Criteria 2 "deceitfulness, as indicated by repeated lying, use of aliases, or conning others for personal profit or pleasure." (Watts 27-29)
  - Criteria 3 "is impulsivity, failure to plan ahead" (Watts 27-15).
  - Criteria 4 "irritability and aggressiveness as

indicated by repeated physical fights or assaults."
(27-19). He doesn't want to be touched which is
typical of someone who has been sexually abused.
(Watts 27-19).

- Criteria 5 "consistent irresponsibility as indicated
  by repeated failure to sustain consistent work
  behavior or honor financial obligations." (Watts,
  27-20).
- Criteria 6 "lack of remorse." (Watts, 27-21).

- "But the dependency traits are very evident with Mr. Basham
  when you look at his relationship with older, higher
  functioning males. He has difficulty making decisions, he
  needs reassurance from them. I think in looking at the crime
  spree Mr. Basham was on, that was very evident when he
  and Andrea Roddy were left in the hotel and Chad Fulks and
  Tina Severance had left. Almost the panic, the scariness. So,
  he has a very difficult time functioning. He relies upon older
  males to look for guidance." (Watts, 27-22). [Basham was 21
  and Fulks 25].
- "I know it has got to be very frustrating for law enforcement
  officials to deal with him. He is difficult to manage." (Watts
  27-32).
- Dr. Capehart is a psychiatrist at the Federal Bureau of
  Prisons in North Carolina. He did a psychiatric evaluation of
  Mr. Basham for the government. (SC p. 27-124). They
  diagnose according to DSM-IV. Basham's principal diagnosis
  is antisocial personality disorder. He also has substance
  abuse and learning disorder. He has a history of head injury
  and attention deficit hyperactivity disorder (ADHD).
  (Capehart p. 27-181). Antisocial personality disorder is the
  major diagnosis that best explains the majority of Basham's
  behavior, Dr. Capehart testifies. (27-182).
- "If you were to ask what one thing best explains what he is
  like today and what he has been like in the past, that one
  thing is antisocial personality disorder." (Capehart 27-183).
- "You are really looking for three or more of the following of
  numbers a (1) through a (7) that have happened since age 15.
  Point number (1), failure to conform to social norms with

respect to lawful behaviors." (Capehart 27-183).

- Capehart is expert for the prosecution of Basham, and Watts is the expert for the defense, but both agree he has symptoms of antisocial personality disorder. Where they disagree is on what caused the disorder. Capehart and Watts agree on 1 (failure to conform) and 2 (deceitfulness) (Capehart 27-184). Capehart agrees with the rest as well. Criteria 3, that he is impulsive, although he thinks he is capable of planning ahead. (27-186) Criteria 4 is aggressiveness, indicated by repeated physical fights or assaults. Criteria 5 is consistent irresponsibility. Criteria 6 is. [lack of remorse]. Criteria 7 is being indifferent to or rationalizing having hurt, mistreated, or stolen from another. Capehart says there is a lot of evidence that he would fail to take responsibility for his actions. (27-190).

- He also had conduct disorder, an example of which is using a blow gun to hurt cats. (p. 27-192). Dr. Capehart explains that Watts agrees he has these characteristics of antisocial personality disorder, but she thinks they are due to different reasons than he does. (Capehart p. 27-193). He says it's not really treatable. (27-194). Dr. Gourley's (prosecuting expert) tests pretty much agreed with Dr. Brawley's (defense expert)—both neuropsychologists. (Capehart p. 27-197). Capehart does not agree with Watts' diagnosis of dementia (p, 27-200).

- "I think Mr. Basham tends to see the world in terms of things that he wants, and then there is everything else, and he is indifferent to it. With respect to sort of doing things that are true or false, I think he feels justified in doing or saying whatever he wants to do to get something that he wants. Because his view of the world is, there are the things that I want, and the things that I don't care about. And if it is in the category I don't care about, I just don't care. You can do whatever you want with that, I don't care. Well, when you put that in the context of sort of the hallmark of antisocial personality disorder is an ongoing disregard for the rights of other people, where an unrelenting focus on getting what you want, to the extent that it infringes on the rights of others. You know, might put others at the risk of harm. Yes,

I think it is consistent with antisocial personality disorder." (Capehart 27-219-220).

- "He doesn't appear to be willing to take responsibility or show remorse for his actions... he also -- he doesn't seem to want treatment for substance abuse." (Capehart p. 27-223).

- Basham told Dr. Capehart that when he isn't incarcerated, he engages in theft and uses drugs. 27-209.

- "And Brandon Basham approaches her and puts a gun in her side. And, thank God, for Andrea Francis, that Deanna Francis walks up. All of a sudden, the mother comes up, and he walks away." (Gasser in Fulks' closing 21-82).

- "Antisocial personality disorder appears to be associated with low socioeconomic status and urban settings. Concerns have been raised that the diagnosis may, at times, be misapplied to individuals in settings in which seemingly antisocial behavior may be part of a protective survival strategy. In assessing antisocial traits, it is helpful for the clinician to consider the social and economic context in which the behaviors occur." (Capehart, p. 27-235).

- Dr. Brannon, neurologist, beginning at 24-223. At 243, re Basham's history, he determined ADHD, chronic drug use, marijuana, cocaine and LSD, and huffing. (24-244)

- He believes his brain impairs him from reasoning as we do. (Brannon 24-253).

- "I don't know that there is a cause-and-effect, in that anybody who has minimal brain dysfunction is bound at some point in their life to commit bad crimes. I turn it around and say it the other way, if you look at somebody who has minimal brain dysfunction, superimpose upon that all of the substance abuse and injuries that are in Mr. Basham's history, you simply understand. It doesn't mean you excuse it, it doesn't mean you do anything other than understand it. And that is where I am coming from. He has an abnormal exam. His brain doesn't work right." (Brannon 24-290)

- "We see these kids being very high risk end up either in juvenile detention or adult incarceration." (Vogelsang, social worker for the Basham defense, 20-5).

- "I don't think I have ever had a case with this many

records." (Vogelsang 20-154)

- "The note of Dr. Sadiq, he says that "Brandon was brought in, got into an argument with his mother in the lobby, and left." "He," Dr. Sadiq, "called Dr. Delaroche, who had been treating him, and was told, quote, "This patient is a psychopath. There is not much we can do for him." (Vogelsang 20-187).

- "Brandon Basham cares more about getting a pinch of dip of tobacco between his cheek and gum during the morning and afternoon breaks of these proceedings than he does about what he did to 19-year-old Samantha Burns along the banks of the Gyandotte river. He cares more about that high, about that rush than what he did to Alice Donovan on a sunny November day in Conway, South Carolina." (Prosecution's closing arguments 29-42).

- "And the findings of the MMPI that was administered to Mr. Basham on July 25th of 1999, are consistent with a diagnosis of antisocial personality disorder." (Vogelsang, 20-186).

- "Remember what Sharon Watkins said? The day that Kathy came to school was the worst day she ever had in 27 years of teaching". (Defense closing 29-136).

- "Between the time Brandon -- from 1991 until the year 2000, that is nine years, was in 12 different institutions, either being committed because of the result of a court order, or the result of psychiatric problems." (Defense closing argument 29-140).

- "You have heard testimony from Dr. Watts and Dr. Brawley who told you that they were told by Dr. Sanders in Kentucky that Brandon Basham is the most hyperactive child he has ever seen in his entire career." (Defense closing argument 29-140).

- "Antisocial Personality Disorders. Remember and recall all of the evidence and testimony from all of the witnesses and all of the experts and all of the medical records that fits this diagnoses like a glove. Like a glove. And explains his behavior. It explains his behavior during the two weeks he is committing these crimes against Samantha and Alice. It explains his behavior since he has been arrested on these charges." (Prosecution closing in Basham 29-185).

Note: Psychiatrists for both the prosecution (Capehart) and the Defense (Watts) agree that Basham has the symptoms of antisocial personality disorder, which is used interchangeably with psychopathy and sociopathy, and is the disorder that leads to them both being irrational actors. The experts only disagreed on whether he also had brain damage and dementia.

Basham as Follower

- Dr. Donna Schwartz-Watts testifies at the SC trial vol. 26, at p. 107 that: "You can't understand Mr. Basham without understanding his relationship with his codefendant. So, I want to learn as much about Mr. Fulks as I could."
- "I don't think he (Basham) had the ability to plan that attempt. [Escape from Hopkins County Jail]. I think he had some abilities to participate in it, and he clearly did. I talked with officer Arison, Major Schaffer, and also Officer Blair, and no one is of the opinion that he was the chief orchestrator of this plan." (Watts, 27-26).
- "I think that Brandon is a follower." (Vogelsang 20-192).

Police, Guards, & Escapes

Presented as typical of Basham's behavior and how difficult he was to control while in various institutions from age 10 to 20 was this incident on January 23, 1997 in Methodist home followed by other incidents in other institutions:
- "Brandon came out of his room and head-butted staff and attempted to push through staff to get inside another resident's room. He hit staff times three, spit in staffs' face two times. Threatened to kill staff and other residents repeatedly. Kicked staff in groin times one, leg, multiple times. Bit staff during 8:00 p.m. visitation. Scratched staff repeatedly." (Vogelsang 20-179).
- And on February 10th, 1997, for example, Charter Behavioral Health system in Evansville, "Mr. Basham was removed from school for being loud and verbally abusive to staff members. Threatening physical harm to the physical

counselor stating, 'I will kick your fucking ass, mother fucker.' resident placed in locked seclusion, found writing on wall in pencil. Resident hid pencil. When asked to hand it over he stated, 'Fuck you. I am going to hit you, you mother fucker'". (20-180, Vogelsang).

- May 26th of '97, "The patient is combative with staff, hitting at first with fist, kicking at staff, taken to time-out room, kicks staff in groin." (20-182, Vogelsang).

- And on January 11th, 2001, four days before he left that facility, (Western State Hospital) the progress note reflects: "Y'all don't tell me what the fuck to do. I do whatever the fuck I want to. If I want to, I will grab that fan and throw it down the hallway. Or if I want to rip that fucking nurses' station off of its foundation, I will. Reality is, there is not a mother fucker big enough in this facility to stop me. That is reality. Got it"? (20-189, Vogelsang).

- "Mr. Jay, who is a counselor of Mr. Basham. The same Clifford Jay Mr. Basham took a knife and took a swing at his throat when Mr. Jay woke him up. Mr. Basham is a teenager, took that knife, tried to slash Mr. Jay's throat." and then called him from jail and said: "Yes, sir, Mr. C. J., we killed them. Yes, sir, Mr. C. J., we killed them." (Call on Christmas Eve 2002 (Prosecution's closing 29-58)

- "Two things important about what Dr. McFadden said. She said he is one of the worst inmates we ever had to deal with at Just Care." (Prosecutor's closing 29-71).

- "Francis Kirkland is the gentleman that spent 20-plus years in military, deeply in his church, testified about an incident where he took a towel, Mr. Basham being out of the cell, being moved for one reason or another. Mr. Basham is all upset and angry. Approached and assaulted officer Kirkland. He was able, Mr. Basham was able to get out of his handcuffs and cuff officer Kirkland. And he was, in his language, not mine, not officer Kirkland's, you remember officer Kirkland's intensity, 'I can kill you, mother fucker. I will kill you'" (Prosecutor's closing 29-74.)

- "James Smith is one of the guys that had to come down and get Mr. Basham off of Francis Kirkland in 2003. Told you about Mr. Basham throwing fluids. About Mr. Basham taking a swing at him, constant threats. Worse inmate he ever had to deal with at Alvin S. Glenn Detention. Lee James, ex-military, somebody used to dealing with young men. Officer Lee said hoarding and getting contraband out of Brandon Basham's cell. Mr. Lee said he was the only inmate ever to lay a hand on him the entire time he has been there. Francis Kirkland, in the 11 years he has been at the detention facility, no one has ever done to him what Brandon Basham did to him on December 31." (Prosecutor's closing 29-75.)

- "Officer Dash said in his eight years at the detention facility, Brandon Basham is the worst inmate he ever had to deal with." (Prosecutor's closing 29-76.)
- "Officer Shellie Anderson . . .told you that he has worked nine-and-a-half years in the federal bop (Bureau of Prisons) as a correctional officer in the North Carolina prison systems. He said it was the most force and the longest period of time it took him ever to get an inmate (Basham) under control in nine-and-a-half years working with inmates in the North Carolina state and federal system." (Prosecutors' closing 29-78).
- "Brandon Basham was hitting his head on the floor and hitting his head against the wall. Ladies and gentlemen, three big guys were able to get Brandon Basham down to the ground." (Defense closing 29-121).
- "I think one that we might not necessarily think as being part of antisocial personality disorder are the actual times he has escaped from some kind of a facility, and the times he has actually attempted to escape from a facility. I think that shows a tremendous disregard for, really, societal norms. I counted five times on the record that he has left." (Capehart 27-219-220).

Mitigating Circumstances

Judge in Basham's SC trial at Vol 29, pp 22-27:   After each factor, the jury vote from Vol 39 beginning at p 8 are listed below in bold. If they did not vote for it, it does not mean that they did not agree that the factor existed, but rather that it should not be considered as a mitigating circumstance in his guilt or innocence.

The statutory mitigating factors alleged in this case which you must consider are:

- One, Impaired capacity. Brandon Leon Basham's capacity to appreciate the wrongfulness of his conduct or to conform his conduct to the requirements of law was significantly impaired, regardless of whether the capacity was so impaired as to constitute a defense to the charge. **6**

- Two, Duress. Brandon Leon Basham was under unusual and substantial duress, regardless of whether the duress was of such a degree as to constitute a defense to the charge. **0**

- Three, Minor participation. Brandon Leon Basham is punishable as a principal in the offense, which was committed by another, but his participation was relatively minor, regardless of whether the participation was so minor as to constitute a defense to the charge. **0**

- Four, Brandon Leon Basham did not have a significant prior history of other criminal conduct. **0**

- Number Five, disturbance. Brandon Leon Basham committed the offense under severe mental or emotional disturbance. **1**

- Number six, any other factors in Brandon Leon Basham's background, record, or character, or any other circumstance of the offense that mitigates it against the imposition of the death sentence. (Nothing stated).

- In addition to the statutory mitigating factors, the defendant asserts a number of non-statutory mitigating factors. These are:

- Number one, Brandon Leon Basham played a lesser role than Chadrick Evan Fulks in the kidnapping and carjacking of Alice Donovan. **0**

- Number two, Brandon Leon Basham's family,

including both his maternal and paternal sides, has a history of violence; substance abuse; mental illness, including schizophrenia; psychosis; depression; delusions; paranoia; and suicide, including numerous suicide attempts by Brandon's mother. **12**

- Number three, Brandon Leon Basham's mother abused alcohol and illegal drugs while she was pregnant with him and had a negative attitude towards prenatal care. **8**

- Four, Brandon Leon Basham's parents spent most of the family money on drugs and alcohol, and Brandon frequently saw both parents intoxicated or under the influence. **8**

- Five, Brandon's mother entertained strange men at her home for drugs and sex, sometimes kicking Brandon, Jimmy, and Charlotte out of the house on such occasions, and sometimes allowing the family to remain, resulting in Brandon occasionally seeing his mother involved with these strange men. **7**

- Six, Brandon Basham was sexually abused by men. **7**

- Seven, Brandon Basham's parents often engaged in physical, verbal, and emotional violence towards each other and towards Brandon and his sister, Charlotte. **12**

- Eight, Brandon Leon Basham's parents did not know how to take care of a special-needs child and never concerned themselves with his education or treatment. **0**

- Nine, Brandon Basham's parents and family failed to show up for visits or conferences at hospitals and institutions. **0**

- Ten, Brandon Leon Basham had inconsistent and inefficient nutrition provided to him in his home. **0**

- Eleven, Brandon Basham's home was often filthy and infected with roaches. **0**

- Twelve, Brandon Basham's mother removed him from appropriate care facilities, refused to follow recommendations of doctors and counselors, and refused to give him his prescribed medicine for his mental illness, but gave him illegal drugs instead. **10**
- Thirteen, Brandon Basham's mother encouraged him to steal to support their drug habits. **12**
- Fourteen, Brandon Basham began huffing gasoline, smoking marijuana, and smoking crack cocaine at a young age. **12**
- Fifteen, Brandon Basham was diagnosed with ADHD, attention deficit hyperactivity disorder, as a young child, was placed in a mental hospital for the first time at age 10, and was subsequently placed in several mental health facilities and institutions. **2**
- Sixteen, Brandon Basham has received inconsistent care and has been prescribed an ever-changing mix of medicines, including antipsychotics, anxiolytics, anti-depressants, and anticonvulsants. **3**
- Seventeen, Brandon Basham suffers from emotional, behavioral, and learning disabilities, and was placed in special education classes in early elementary school. **0**
- Eighteen, Brandon Basham shows signs of neurological damage, due to head trauma and substance abuse, which has inhibited his ability to process information and inhibit impulses. **0**
- Nineteen, Brandon Basham suffers from dementia, due to multiple etiologies, inhalant-induced psychosis with hallucinations, and anxiety disorder, not otherwise specified, and ADHD, combined type. **1**
- Twenty, Brandon Basham has a mental condition that causes him to reject prescribed medications and self-medicate with other non-prescribed substances, such as illegal drugs and alcohol. **0**

- Twenty-one, Brandon Basham is unable to operate a car, an ATM machine, or a phone card. **0**
- Twenty-two, Brandon Basham has suffered from low self-esteem, sadness, and hopelessness from a young age. **0**
- Twenty-three, Brandon Basham has attempted suicide several times. **0**
- Twenty-four, Brandon Basham's intelligence scores have been deteriorating ·due to his head injuries and substance abuse at an early age, and his IQ level is now in the low seventies. **0**
- Twenty-five, Brandon Basham is easily influenced and led by others. **6**
- Twenty-six, at the time of the offenses, Brandon Basham was suffering from severe mental and emotional disturbances. **0**
- Twenty-seven, at the time of the offenses, Brandon Basham was not on his prescribed medication. **0**
- Twenty-eight, at the time of the offenses, Brandon Basham was under the influence of alcohol and drugs. **0**
- Twenty-nine, Brandon Basham has never harmed anyone in a correctional facility, with or without a weapon. **0**
- Thirty, no one has escaped from a high-security federal prison since 1993. (Judge in jury instructions in Basham 29-222-227). **0**

(End juror vote on mitigating factors in Basham, vol. 30-8-9).

We, the jury, as to Brandon Leon Basham, unanimously find beyond a reasonable doubt that the aggravating factors proved in this case outweigh the mitigating factors so as to justify a sentence of death. Or in the absence of any mitigating factor, that the aggravating factor or factors alone justify a sentence of death. We, therefore, unanimously conclude that Brandon Leon Basham shall be sentenced to death. (30-9).

The factors that all twelve members of the jury agreed were mitigating were:

- Two, Brandon Leon Basham's family, including both his maternal and paternal sides, has a history of violence; substance abuse; mental illness, including schizophrenia; psychosis; depression; delusions; paranoia; and suicide, including numerous suicide attempts by Brandon's mother. **12**
- Seven, Brandon Basham's parents often engaged in physical, verbal, and emotional violence towards each other and towards Brandon and his sister, Charlotte. **12**
- Thirteen, Brandon Basham's mother encouraged him to steal to support their drug habits. **12**
- Fourteen, Brandon Basham began huffing gasoline, smoking marijuana, and smoking crack cocaine at a young age. **12**

These factors go to his psychopathy of being raised in violence, seeing it, experiencing it, and being coached into it, in addition to using drugs.

Extraordinary Criminals

Bonding

It is not just about the deficiencies in their individual pasts, but how they bonded, based upon those common deficiencies. They were placed together as cellmates and what apparently drew them together was a common, similar background with shared life experiences, values, violence, drugs, and stealing in their pasts. Once they escaped from jail together, and embarked upon their crime spree together, they had nothing to lose. Their similarities included the following characteristics:

- They were both of the crime committing age group of 18-25. Fulks was 25, Basham was 21.
- They were both white males.
- They had similar IQs that were below average, somewhere

between 65 and 75.

- They grew up in similar geographic areas in and around Kentucky and West Virginia.
- They both had alcoholic fathers and alcoholic or drug-addicted mothers.
- They had both attempted suicide as teenagers.
- They both saw physical fights between their parents and saw their parents divorced.
- They were both physically abused as children by their parents.
- They were both sexually abused as children by older men.
- They were both raised in poor and/or disadvantaged situations economically.
- They were both taught how to be violent by a brother, uncle, or parent.
- They were both unemployed. Basham had never worked, Fulks rarely.
- They both were school dropouts with learning disabilities. Basham may have just made it to 7th grade; Fulks the same.
- They both had prior criminal records.
- They both had been institutionalized multiple times and had escaped before.
- Neither were married at the time, but Fulks had already been married twice and was sexually active and violent with women. Basham had not been married, had limited sexual encounters and a sexual identity problem.
- Neither of them had children.
- They were both on illegal drugs from childhood to the present.
- They both committed violence at an early age. Fulks was on probation by age 9.
- The system failed both of them.
- This is trial testimony about their bonding:
    - Dr. Watts wanted to learn about Fulks because with Basham's personality, Chad Fulks is the kind of person Basham would bond with.
    - Basham, because of his intellectual capability and his

dependency on other people, and Fulks with his personality and his background, as far as intellectual functioning and personality, bonded. Fulks is the type of person that Basham would bond with. Historically, Fulks has been the type of person Basham has bonded with. (Attny SC trial, 26-138).

- The two of these men acted together as one in concert with one another. They were a two-man death squad. Two men formed one team. "(Gasser in Fulks' Closing at 20-25).

What makes this crime unforeseeable is just how extraordinarily bad these perpetrators were, even by the standards of people who work with criminals. And no one-- family, friends, the mental health system, the criminal justice system--was ever able to help either one of them. In sum, this is what some of the professionals and family said who came in contact with them or treated them:

Chad Fulks

- *I haven't seen a brain quite as abnormal as that (of Fulks)—neurologist for defense in criminal trial.* (Neuroscientist, Dr. Ruben Gur, in Fulks' criminal trial).
- *The most remarkable thing is his mother doesn't remember when he was born, and his father doesn't remember him at all* until Chad was 12, and they all lived in the same house—Social Worker Andrews for defense in criminal trial.
- *Dewayne Fulks, Chad's brother, said the police referred to their little blue house on the corner so often that his dad painted the house yellow.*
- *Here is a man (Fulks) who has beaten and physically abused just about every woman in his life.* (Prosecuting attorney in Fulks criminal trial.)
- "I wish I could have taken him because I feel like the whole system failed him and that their family was ignored". Chad's aunt, Gayle Beatty, at SC Trial.
- I think we can safely say this. If Chad Fulks had been

removed from the home when Sue Hatcher's probation officer made the recommendation, along with the police officer and principal, then we wouldn't be here today." (Mr. Blum, Fulks' defense closing).

Basham

- *I've never seen a record of abuse and neglect like this in 20 years*—(the defense attorney for Basham in the criminal trial.)
- *It is one of the worst developmental histories I've seen (Basham's)*—a social worker in criminal trial.
- *He's the most distractible patient in 17 years of practice (Basham).* (Dr. Brawley, forensic neuropsychologist in Basham's defense at trial).
- *One of the most hyperactive individuals I have seen in 11 years of practicing forensic psychiatry (Basham).* (Dr. Watts, social worker for Basham's defense).
- *Basham is the most hyperactive child he has ever seen in his entire career.* (Dr. Sanders from Basham's childhood records).
- *Teacher Sharon Watkins said the day that Kathy (Basham's mother) came to school was the worst day she ever had in 27 years of teaching.*
- *I've never been afraid as I was at that house—social worker re Basham's parents.*
- *Basham is one of the worst inmates we ever had to deal with at Just Care.* (Dr. McFadden, at Just Care facility)
- *Basham is the only inmate to lay a hand on him in my 11 years.* (James Smith at Alvin S. Glenn Detention).
- *Officer Dash says Basham is the worst inmate in his 8 years.*
- *He's psychotic. There's nothing you can do with him.* (Dr. Delaroche who had been treating Basham).
- The agencies and institutions were never effective or helpful to him (Basham). Vogelsang, social worker for defense for Basham).
- The agencies and institutions that we count on to intervene on behalf of a child like Brandon, to act in their behalf

and protect them, never did so in any kind of consistent way, any kind of long-term way, or any kind of way that was effective or helpful to him. (Vogelsang, social work for defense for Basham.

- *I've never had a trial this long.* The Judge in the Basham case.

Prior Crimes of Perpetrators

These perpetrators had prior arrests and convictions, but none were for a violent crime of this nature, where they had perpetrated robbery with injury, rape, or homicide. They were both known to the criminal justice system but were not known to the Huntington Mall. *Business cannot be expected to prevent a crime that the criminal justice system cannot prevent,* [stated by a California State judge several years ago] especially when these are jail escapees who are wanted criminals with warrants for their arrests.

Tina Severance said at trial (SC Vol III, p. 63) that Chad told her he couldn't go back and do time for 60 years, which is why he escaped. He said he couldn't go back to prison. Tina Severance in SC trial Vol III at p. 115, says that the night of the 11th of November, when they left, she assumed they were going to a mall to look for purses and rob things out of cars. She doesn't think they were targeting women's cars. No warning was given to Huntington Mall or the community or to Samantha Burns to be on the lookout for these dangerous criminals. The Huntington Mall is in a bucolic area where people often do not even lock the doors in their houses or their cars. Samantha Burns would not expect such a heinous attack, nor could the Huntington Mall because they were not on notice of an event such as this being imminent.

Subsequent Crimes of Perpetrators

As can be seen from the timeline of the crime spree, Fulks and Basham went on to commit many more crimes after the murder of Samantha Burns until they were caught. In the other locations, they committed similar crimes even in daylight, in the presence of surveillance cameras, and in parking lots with multiple potential witnesses.

Based on the perpetrators' subsequent behavior in carrying out additional crimes, there is no reason to believe that additional measures at the Huntington Mall would have deterred these two criminals. An analysis of their *modus operandi*, especially as seen in the videotape at the Wal-Mart parking lot, is that they were so quick that even if a guard or a witness saw them and their activities, they would not view it as suspicious activity. When they pull in behind the victim (Donovan) at the Wal-Mart lot, Basham is out of the vehicle immediately and into her car, and then they immediately pull out and leave the lot. A passerby (or a guard) would not view it as suspicious and could easily conclude that a boyfriend, husband, or relative, was just dropped off in order to join his girlfriend, wife, or sister.

There was nothing suspicious on the video about their behavior. Similarly, their prior crimes were breaking into cars and stealing from cars. They likely did that in the Burns' abduction as quickly and clandestinely as they did the Donovan abduction from the Wal-Mart lot. In fact, their girlfriends testify to their efficiency in similar crimes that they committed when they were with them during their crime spree.

This event was not foreseeable based on the nature of the crime and the unusual nature of the perpetrators. And, as the Judge stated at the WV sentencing of Fulks, "This was a random abduction of Samantha."

How Rare These Crimes Are

The unusual nature of the crime and the unusual nature of the criminals made this crime unforeseeable. In Basham's criminal trial, the prosecuting attorney said to Charlotte Basham--Brandon's sister: "You and Brandon were raised in the same environment, and you turned out okay." But this is the part that people have the most difficulty understanding. Siblings can be raised in the same environment and turn out differently. Why? Because it is never the *same*. Birth order makes a difference, sex of the siblings makes a difference, genetics make a difference, and environment makes a difference. Like in Charlotte's case, she says that she (fortunately) turned out more like her father (a quiet, hard-working alcoholic) than her mother (an aggressive, in-your-face, drug addict).

More importantly, the answer to the attorney's question about why she turned out okay, and Brandon did not, is that 90% of all violence is perpetrated by men, not women, and particularly stranger-to-stranger violence. Throughout all societies, throughout all of history, including today in the United States, violence is perpetrated primarily by men, and men are also more likely to be the victims of violence.

- This crime was unusual because females are much less likely to be victimized than men.
- This crime was unusual because females are much more likely to be killed by someone they know than by a stranger.
- This crime was unusual because it is rare to have a death in a rape.
- This crime was unusual because it is not likely to have death in a robbery. If there is death in a robbery, it is most likely because there was resistance, not an explanation in this case.
- This crime is unusual because it was part of a murder spree, and less than 2% of murders are as a result of serial murderers, mass murderers, or spree murderers.

How Bad These Perpetrators Were

It was not just that Fulks and Basham were bad, it is that were extraordinarily bad. It is not just that one of them was a psychopath, it is that they were both psychopaths. It is not just that they were psychopaths, but that they were psychopaths operating together. It is not just that they operated together, but that they bonded. They bonded on a murder spree over a time span of 17 days and geography of seven states that left death, carnage, and devastated families in their wake. This is the kind of crime spree that you see on a television series or movie or read about in a crime novel, this is not the kind of crime spree that you expect to happen in Huntington, West Virginia. But it is also the kind of crime spree that you could not make up because reality in this case was much worse than fiction, and the actors were much worse in real life than any writer could create. Staff from their respective institutions said they were the worst they had ever seen.

The Making of Psychopathic Killers

Childhood circumstances, social background, and violence can combine to create a psychopath. Both Fulks and Basham are classic psychopaths. Fulks was diagnosed with antisocial personality disorder in 1998. Basham was diagnosed with antisocial personality disorder in 1999 and later by Dr. Watts and Dr. Capehart. Only three or more of the five official DSM-IV symptoms of Antisocial Personality Disorder are needed to be classified as a psychopath. Fulks and Basham both had all five symptoms. They have them now, they had them at the time of the crime, and they had them in childhood. They are:
1. failure to conform to social norms;
2. deceitfulness and lying;
3. impulsivity;
4. irritability and aggressiveness;
5. reckless disregard for safety of self or others.
Robert Hare's list of 20 psychopathic features that I have used on the other serial killers also fits this pair. Consider the evidence from interviews with family and friends, mental and medical evaluations, statements from prison guards, social workers, doctors, neuroscientists, neurologists, and radiologists in assessing each one to see if the glove fits, and it does. The glove fits Fulks. The glove fits Basham. This is the list with some examples of how they fit each category.

Chad Fulks and Donald Basham **Psychopathy Check List**
√ GLIB and SUPERFICIAL CHARM √ GRANDIOSE SELF-WORTH √ NEED FOR STIMULATION or PRONENESS TO BOREDOM √ PATHOLOGICAL LYING √ CONNING AND MANIPULATIVENESS √ LACK OF REMORSE OR GUILT √ SHALLOW √ CALLOUSNESS and LACK OF EMPATHY √ PARASITIC LIFESTYLE √ POOR BEHAVIORAL CONTROLS √ PROMISCUOUS SEXUAL BEHAVIOR √ EARLY BEHAVIOR PROBLEMS √ LACK OF REALISTIC, LONG-TERM GOALS √ IMPULSIVITY √ IRRESPONSIBILITY √ FAILURE TO ACCEPT RESPONSIBILITY FOR OWN ACTIONS √ MANY SHORT-TERM MARITAL RELATIONSHIPS √ JUVENILE DELINQUENCY √ REVOCATION OF CONDITION RELEASE √ CRIMINAL VERSATILITY √ = The item applies to both Basham and Fulks. No check mark indicates it does not apply or information was not available to make an informed decision.

As with James Wood, I had the childhood histories of Fulks and Basham and their trials. They, like Woods, had every item apply to them as psychopaths, shown in the table above. Below, the examples are given for each factor.

1) Glib and superficial charm
   - Women and girls were charmed by them, even after they knew they were murderers, and the female guard at Hopkins aided in their escape.
2) Grandiose self-worth
   - In spite of their lack of IQ, education, job skills, and viable relationships, they did not manifest or express low self-esteem.
3) Need for stimulation or proneness to boredom
   - Basham especially needed constant stimulation, was very edgy, and according to his sister, extremely annoying from the time he was two years old. Dr. Watts says Basham acts as if he's driven by a motor. Fulks was the leader in the spree, constantly on the run, and moving from place to place.
4) Pathological lying
   - Their lying from childhood was very extreme, and they lied to every law enforcement officer to whom they spoke. They were constantly changing their stories, admitting that they had lied in the previous story, and then would just continue lying.
5) Conning and manipulativeness
   - Basham stole from the time he was two, according to his sister. He would steal her jewelry, and he and his mother would pawn it for money. She couldn't take him to perform in the Special Olympics because she was afraid he would steal from everyone there. Fulks' own grandmother would not let him come over because he would steal from her. Fulks and Basham had always made their livings by stealing from others.
6) Lack of remorse or guilt
   - There is no indication from their childhoods that they showed remorse or guilt. The most disturbing observations from the trial records are that they never showed remorse or guilt, throughout their trials, even during the victim impact statements.

7) Shallow affect
- They both had a limited and shallow range of feeling, with no depth. No matter how much you read from all of the work-ups and evaluations that were done on them, there is no indication that they ever care. What they did to the victim in this case is unspeakable.

8) Callousness and lack of empathy
- They are both cold and inconsiderate, and they used people without concern for their feelings. They left Tina and Andrea stranded in a motel in South Carolina, with no money or car. The FBI had to give the girls money to get back home.

9) Parasitic lifestyle
- They were always financially dependent on someone else. They stole checks, credit cards, jewelry, and ATM cards from people and used them as their own. They had always lived off of women and relatives. Basham was in jail for stealing from his own father.

10) Poor behavioral controls
- They constantly displayed erratic behavior, whether it was Basham attacking guards in prison, or Fulks beating up every woman in his life.

11) Promiscuous sexual behavior
- They both exhibited promiscuous sexual behavior. Fulks was in multiple relationships at once over the years. His second wife said he wanted sex (rough sex) six to ten times a day. Basham was in bed with Fulks' friend Beth McGuffin minutes after he met her. He apparently tried to fondle cellmates.

12) Early behavior problems
- The record is rife with examples of their early behavior problems, many prior to age 13, including lying, theft, cheating, glue-sniffing, alcohol and drug use, running away from home, and suicide attempts.

13) Lack of realistic, long-term goals
- They had no long-term goals. They obviously had no idea after they escaped from prison what they were going to do, or where they were going to go. Fulks just instinctively went back to every place he knew. One of

the attorneys at the criminal trial said "Wouldn't you think they would at least go someplace new?"

14) Impulsivity

- They did not consider the consequences of their actions and were always erratic and reckless to the end, when Fulks tried to run over and outrun law enforcement, and Basham shot at law enforcement.

15) Irresponsibility

- Stealing to live is the primary example of their irresponsibility. That's what Dewayne says he taught Chad to do, and Brandon's mother, by example, stole cats and dogs from neighbors and sold them for drugs.

16) Failure to accept responsibility for own actions

- Nothing was ever their fault. An attorney at trial referred to their TODDI defense, which is that "The Other Dude Did It". Fulks and Basham blame each other. They will not tell the truth about who did what to which victim or where the victims can be found.

17) Many short-term marital relationships

- Fulks lived with a 30-year old woman when he was 15-years-old, and had already been married twice, and he was only 25. Basham had not had as much time for relationships, since he was only 21, but he masturbated in front of nurses in jail and was considered "queer" by fellow inmates. At age 7, he said he wanted to be a male stripper.

18) Juvenile delinquency

- Basham knew nothing else but the inside of state hospitals and prisons for his juvenile years, and Fulks was on probation from the time he was nine. Their crimes started when they were five or six years old.

19) Revocation of conditional release

- They did not just revoke probation, they escaped from jail, and they had done it before, even before they escaped from the jail, preceding the crime spree at issue.

20) Criminal versatility

- They committed all kinds of crimes, and psychopaths particularly take pride in getting away with it, as did they. Fulks and Basham did a lot of crimes, but their specialty was stealing from cars, and Fulks had an affinity for Walmarts. They even stole from each other during the crime spree.

Coaching Them into Violence

It is not just being raised in a bad environment that makes a person a violent criminal. It is the coaching into violence that is believed to create violence. Three things are needed: 1) seeing violence, 2) experiencing violence, and 3) being coached into violence. Both Fulks and Basham saw their parents physically fight each other. Both Fulks and Basham as children were beaten by their parents, particularly by their mothers, and both Fulks and Basham were coached into violence—Fulks was coached by his brother, Dewayne, and Basham was coached by his mother.

Irrational Actors

Their individual childhood environments, social backgrounds, and violence led them to become the psychopaths and irrational actors they are today. Irrational actors because of their mental condition and/or drugs are simply not deterrable through ordinary measures. Fulks and Basham were also risk-takers, who did not consider the consequences of their actions. The Hopkins County Jail could not--indeed did not--contain them. In fact, that jail is where the trouble began as far as the psychopathic pair going on this crime spree.

Basham could not keep a cellmate, but when he was placed with Fulks, two weeks before their escape, the complaints stopped. There is no record that Fulks asked for a new cellmate. Why would he? He and Basham shared the kind of background that made them a perfect match. They not only shared similar backgrounds, but they had a shared value system. Once they escaped, they had already determined they were not going back. Basham was prepared to kill cops to keep from going back, he said, and Fulks said he wasn't going back because with his new child abuse charge, he would be doing long, hard time. Those are the two psychopathic, irrational actors that engaged in the crime spree that began when they broke the fence to freedom from

Hopkins County Jail at 8 PM on Monday night, November 4th, 2002.

Basham and Fulks both fit the criteria of psychopaths (antisocial personality disorder) who were on a murder spree. Both were raised in the most difficult of childhood circumstances. Both had intellectual and emotional disabilities, exacerbated by the use of illegal drugs. Both were surrounded by violence from childhood on. They saw violence, they experienced violence, and they in turn perpetrated violence upon others. And no one, in the family or in the system, saved them. Mental institutions and jails could not hold them.

If a combined 40 years of attempts to stop their crimes, in over twenty institutions in several states failed, how could the Huntington Mall stop them? It is my opinion that even if a security guard had been patrolling in the mall in a security vehicle, in a well-lit parking lot, it would not have prevented this crime because a security guard would be no match for the likes of Fulks and Basham.

After the criminal trials, I visited the mall, where Samantha was abducted. It looks like any mall USA, so there is little to report from that visit. What there is to report is the astonishing life of these perpetrators, even in the aftermath of the killings and after their convictions. They were sentenced to life in prison and sent to Federal Prisons. As I am writing this, it has been fifteen years (in 2002), since they committed their crimes, and they are both still awaiting execution. For a time, Fulks was on a website. It was called www.deathrowspeaks.com Below, I include an interview from that web-site; this from one of the worst killers this country has ever seen. These photos are taken from www.mylifeofcrime.wordpress.com 4/16/2017.

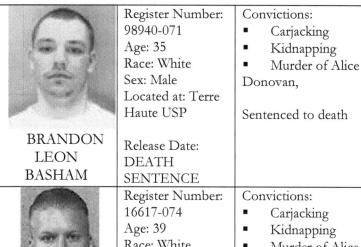

	Register Number: 98940-071 Age: 35 Race: White Sex: Male Located at: Terre Haute USP Release Date: DEATH SENTENCE	Convictions: • Carjacking • Kidnapping • Murder of Alice Donovan, Sentenced to death
BRANDON LEON BASHAM		
CHADRICK EVAN FULKS	Register Number: 16617-074 Age: 39 Race: White Sex: Male Located at: Terre Haute USP Release Date: DEATH SENTENCE	Convictions: • Carjacking • Kidnapping • Murder of Alice Donovan, Sentenced to death

Brandon Basham Death Row Interview

My name is Brandon Basham. I'm 24 years old and am currently the youngest person on Federal death row. I've been here for a year and it's a real lonely place. I am originally from the State of Kentucky. Was born and raised there. I am a single white guy, never married and I've not fathered any children. These are things which I think about a lot. I'll likely never have an opportunity to experience a normal life on the outside. That's a depressing and disturbing prospect.

I spend my time here doing things in order to occupy my mind, body and spirit. I love to read, including self-help, spiritual and educational books. For pleasure I read books by Stephen King, John Grisham and many others. I love watching movies on TV and listening to music on my Walkman.

I stay in tip top physical shape by working out three to five times a week. I do exercises for strength, endurance and for cardiovascular health. We aren't allowed to lift weights, do pull-ups, etc. so I'm required to get creative with my workout program. My physical description is: Solid, athletic build with great muscle tone, 5' 10" 192 pounds, brown hair and eyes.

I have many interests including beaches, the outdoors, swimming, cycling, nature, meeting new people and living life to the fullest when possible.

I am the youngest of two children. My sister is several years older than me. I'm fortunate to have her and my niece in my life. Our mother died this past July (2005) which has left a void in my heart. I also am thankful to have friends. I hope that someone reading this profile will decide to write me. Receiving mail from those of you on the outside would mean a lot. I promise to answer all letters promptly. Thanks for reading about me. Address: Brandon Basham, Reg. No. 98940-071, USP-Terre Haute, PO Box 12015, Terre-Haute, IN 47801, USA. Brandon Basham, Federal Death Row, April 16, 2017 [End Basham Death Row Interview].

A jury recommended the death sentence for the 2002 kidnapping and murder of a 44-year-old-white South Carolina woman following Fulks' escape from a Kentucky jail. Fulks' codefendant, Brandon Basham, was tried in September 2004 for crimes committed during the escape. Fulks was the first federal death conviction in South Carolina.

Chadrick Evan Fulks

Interviews with the Condemned, Interview no. 18 (2006-07-03). Interview nr.18 is being held with Chadrick Evan Fulks. Chadrick is fairly new on the federal death row unit at Terre Haute, and I don't know too much about him either. Please read this interview below to learn a little more about him. We would like to thank Chadrick for his time and effort to answer our questions and to participate with this interview series.

Chadrick Fulks Death Row Interview

Personality: Name: Chadrick Evan Fulks, Prison Register: 16617-074, Address: USP Terre Haute, PO Box 12015, Terre Haute, IN. 47801, Age: 28, Race: White, Sex: Male, How long on Death Row: 2 years

1: Question: Where were you born and raised?

Answer: I was born in a little town called Lincoln County West Virginia and I moved to Huntington West Virginia around the age of 2 and was raised there until the age of 13.

2: Question: Will you share with us what it was like for you growing up? (Did you have a pet, a favorite game, hiding place, or favorite toy? Were you raised by both parents, a single parent, or relative?)

Answer: Well, growing up was hard for me, but I'll do my best to explain it to you. First of all I loved animals. I would always take in all of the stray dogs and cats I found and I would hide them in the basement of our house and feed them whatever I could. But one dog I remember best was our Poodle "Prissy." We had her for 15 years and she was so protective of all of the family. I can remember when things were bad at home and we kids would hide behind the couch or outside, Prissy would be right there with us to protect us and she didn't weigh 10 pounds.

My favorite game was "hide n seek." I can remember me and my brothers and 2 cousins playing it all of the time. My favorite toy was a remote control car my mom and dad got me for Christmas: it was a grey Corvette, the kind with a wire to the control. And my favorite hiding place was behind the couch in the living room. My mom and dad stayed together until I was 13 then my mom and dad divorced and my mom was left with all 5 of us kids, but I raised myself from the age of 14, I lived on my own wherever I could.

3: Question: Do you have a favorite childhood memory? If so, what is it?

Answer: Yes I do; it was when my mom gave her life to God and quit drinking, smoking and fighting.

4: Question: Did you like school? If so, share with us your favorite memory from your school years.

Answer: School was very hard for me because I had a speech problem and I never had nice clothes so the kids always made fun of me. But I do have a favorite memory. It was when my youngest brother and I joined the football team together. Although it didn't last long, it was special to me because it was me and my little brother together.

5: Question: What person or event impacted you most as a child?

Answer: I would have to say my parents' divorce, and also seeing my mom give her life to God.

6: Question: What hobbies or activities did you participate in while growing up, e.g. scouting, sports, etc.?

Answer: The only thing was playing football for three weeks. I also learned how to build cars and motors by watching my dad. I also got certified as a welder.

7: Question: What was your first job? Please describe your duties/responsibilities and whether or not you liked the job.

Answer: My first real job was at McGinnis Barge Company in South Point Ohio. I was a welder and I did Barge repair on River Barges. I loved it, welding was like a sport to me.

8: Question: As a child or teenager, what did you want to do when you grew up? Why?

Answer: As a child I wanted to be a doctor but as I got into my late teens I wanted to be a counselor for kids who was going through what I did as a child. Why? Because I wanted to make sure no one, no kid, ever had to feel what I felt and never had to get through what I did.

9: Question: Do you have a favorite movie or book? Please elaborate.

Answer: My favorite movie is Saving Private Ryan and Full Metal Jacket because it gave me some idea what my dad went through in Vietnam and why he done the things he did, it helped me understand that it mentally changed him and it wasn't by choice.

10: Question: Where was the most beautiful or special place that you can remember having visited? Please describe it.

Answer: It is the Blue Ridge Mountains in West Virginia. I'll never forget it!! There is a sightseeing place that looks over the mountains and a river ran through it and as it was getting late I looked over and saw why it's called the Blue Ridge Mountains. The mountain was blue and the sparkles were coming from the river, it stole my breath. I have a picture of me there, I'll send it to you.

11: Question: What is the funniest thing that ever happened to you?

Answer: Me and my brother Ronnie were walking to my uncle's house and decided to take a short cut across a cow pasture. My brother starts waving a shirt at what we thought was a cow and we were chased and I got stuck in a tree. It turned out that cow was really a bull and he wasn't going to let me out of the tree so I was stuck in that tree for a while.

12: Question: What job or occupation did you have prior to your incarceration? Were you employed at the time of your arrest?

Answer: I was a welder for Coachman RV's in Middle Berry Indiana building aluminum frames for the inside structure of the walls in the RV's. And I lost this job 4 months before I was arrested on this charge.

13: Question: Were you involved with drugs or alcohol prior to your incarceration? If so, please share the effects this had on your life.

Answer: Yes, I was on Meth, cocaine, weed and drunk daily. The effect it had on me is overwhelming, it tore my life apart. Meth is the devil's drug; it will get a hold of you and rip you apart. I lost everything I had and it is a big reason I am here today. It takes your ability to think away and you don't even realize the stuff that is going on around you and in my case I was so worried about smoking Meth that I didn't even take the time to stop and realize that I was tearing other people's lives apart by stealing from them to be able to afford to get this drug. It tore the bond I did have with my family apart and I'll never forgive myself for that.

14: Question: What do you miss most about the outside world and why?

Answer: Freedom, the beauty of nature, and the freedom of being able to be with my family is what I miss most. I love to be around people and being able to help people when in need. I miss being a son, a brother, a father, a husband, and a friend. I miss having a life.

15: Question: What is the one thing you regret most?

Answer: I regret a lot of things but the one that sticks out the most is putting my mom through all of this. And escaping from prison in 2002.

16: Question: Do you have any strong spiritual or religious beliefs? If so do they influence how you view the future?

Answer: I am a Pentecostal and I believe that God is the one who knows I never took the lives of these victims I'm accused of killing and I believe the truth shall set you free. I know God will not let me die for something I didn't do.

17: Question: How important is it for you to have contact

with your family, friends and/or the outside world? Please elaborate.

Answer: It is the most important thing; I know from experience that without family and friends on the outside that it will drive you crazy. I recently dropped my appeal because I couldn't do this alone but God sent me an angel in disguise to help me through this and I picked it back up so I believe that having contact with the outside world is vital.

18: Question: Do you remember your first thoughts when hearing the jury's verdict of death as your sentence? Will you share this experience with us, e.g. your thoughts, feelings, reactions?

Answer: Well, I felt what they were going to say long before the verdict due to the fact that the government and the judge only gave me jurors who favored the death penalty, but I still wasn't prepared to hear the verdict of death, I just couldn't believe it was really happening. I was mad, sad, shocked, confused, and I can remember just asking God to be with my mom as she heard this. She was my biggest concern because I knew it was going to tear her apart. I couldn't believe the Government would sentence someone to death that didn't even commit the murder. And I kept thinking that this just wasn't real.

19: Question: What is a typical day like for you on death row?

Answer: It's a struggle. I sit here in a 6x13 cell 162 hours a week. I look at pictures of my family a lot and I sit and write to my family even though my mom is the only one who writes back. I work out (push-ups and sit-ups). I write poems and I wait for mail call hoping for mail and that's about it I can tell you. These are some long hard days.

20: Question: Do you feel that capital punishment serves as a deterrent? Yes/No please elaborate on your answer.

Answer: No I believe capital punishment is murder any way you look at it. I don't believe taking someone's life for a crime they're accused of admitting is the right way. No one has the right to take a human life whether it's a citizen or the U.S. government.

21: Question: If you could change one thing in the world today, what would it be and why?

Answer: It would be how the legal system is conducted and ran because it's just as guilty of breaking the law as anyone, but they get away with it. They can sentence innocent people to death and carry it out. And it's called Justice or a mistake (executed innocent's), but with anyone else it's murder.

22: Question: If you could go back in time, where and to what date would you travel and why?

Answer: I would go back to Huntington West Virginia to November 1995 because that's when my 6 month old son died. I just believe I could have done something to save him because I know if he would have never died and I would be home with him and I'd never be here.

See, my ex-wife and I would take turns on getting up in the morning with him and the morning he died was my morning to sleep in. If I would have gotten up with Devon that morning he would be alive today.

23: Question: What has been the most important and life-altering event you have experienced?

Answer: Losing my son in 1995 and being sentenced to death in 2003 for 2 murders I didn't commit.

24: Question: What is the most important thing that you want our visitors to know about you?

Answer: That I'm not a murderer and that I'm human, I do have a heart. I will not give up until the truth is out, I did not kill these people. I took 3 PolyGram tests by the FBI and passed all 3 but wasn't able to let my jurors know I took and passed these lie detector tests. The government denied me the right to do that. And that I'm willing to work with anyone who wants to help me prove the truth and to help locate the victims remains for some closure for their loved one.

25: Question: If you have anything else that you would like included as a part of this interview, please share it with us now.

Answer: Please work to abolish the death penalty. I would like to ask for anyone willing to help in my case to please contact me. I also want to thank the Angel God sent into my life. Thank you for a chance to share this part of my life it wasn't easy but it needs to come out. [End of Fulk's Death Row Interview].

Early on in the civil suit, Arnie and I had visited the Huntington Mall with my lawyer. This time when I said, "Let's get out of here", it was for a different reason than being in a dangerous area. It was so non-descript and "safe" that there was nothing to see. The civil case was settled and did not go to trial.

CHAPTER TWELVE

~

IS ANY PLACE SAFE?

Over twenty-five years of expert witnessing and working on over 200 cases has made me wonder if any place is safe. The cases in this book make the same point about the serial killers. You never know where or whom they are going to strike. A summary of those four cases showed that clearly:

- The victims were engaged in normal, routine activities, such as shopping, getting gas, sleeping, working, or drinking out.
- The victims were geographically spread from the East to Midwest to the Southwest: West Virginia, Missouri, Iowa, and New Mexico.
- The women were murdered by stabbing, shooting, and/or strangulation and were raped either before or after their murders.
- The women were alone.
- The perpetrators were all white males.
- The victims were white (one was Hispanic/white).
- The male perpetrators ranged in age from 21-46.
- The female victims were from 19 to 36.
- Serial killers are typically white, young males, which the serial killers were.
- The serial killers operated alone; the spree killers worked together—Fulks and Basham--with Fulks as the leader and Basham as the follower.
- The locations included these venues: shopping mall, service station, hotel, and a convenience store.

In my other civil suits, venues where violent crimes have occurred have included the following:

- Sports stadiums
- Banks
- Hospitals
- Convenience stores
- Parking garages
- Apartments
- Motels
- Hotels
- Bars and Clubs
- Nursing homes
- Guard companies
- Taxi cabs
- Work-out rooms
- Strip malls
- Casinos
- Grocery stores
- Fast Food
- Service stations
- Schools
- Retail stores
- Businesses
- Flower stands
- Espresso stands
- Condominiums
- Concert venues

My cases are not statistically representative of crime in general because you can only sue, if there is someone to sue, like a business. For that reason, I do not see violent crime reported by homeowners, even though the most frequent place for violent crime is in the home or on the streets and highways. In addition, you are also more likely to be killed by someone you know than by a stranger, but domestic cases are unlikely to end up as a civil suit. One of the most interesting aspects of these is that these were most violent ones, and they were all committed by serial killers. They happened in the early 1990s, when crime was at its height, and crime has been decreasing, for the most part, since that time. The criminal violence, and resulting civil cases, occur everywhere geographically too, which you can see, in the discussion of cases below.

For various reasons, some cases strike you harder than others. Arnie summarizes some of these cases [fictional names and places], below, that stand out for him by the suddenness and random nature of the events.

A Casino Murder

In Las Vegas, Marian Haines, stepped off the Strip into a casino at 0200am, taking only three steps before being hit in the neck by a 9mm bullet, killing her instantly. There had been two bucket thieves stealing coins from patrons playing the slots. Usually, the bucket thieves are relatively harmless and unarmed, but not this time. A young female guard attempted to stop one of them, and a heavy set guard piled on top of the other. The bucket thief pulled a gun, and shot the guard through the stomach. Another shot rang out and hit Marian, whizzing right past a slots player, who never even saw it, but you see it on camera. That civil case went to trial. There was no one there from Marian's family because she had only her 90-year-old grandparents, and they lived in Hawaii and could not travel to Las Vegas. Rosemary testified as defense for the trial, in the early 2000s, and the verdict was for the casino—that they could not have foreseen such an event.

A Deadly Drive-Through

In the 2000s, one night, a young mother, was holding her 4-year-old child in the passenger seat of a pick-up truck at a pass-thru at a fast food restaurant . A 22-caliber bullet was fired from a gun, shot by a "wanna-be" gang member inside of the restaurant. The bullet traveled through the dining room, kitchen, pass through booth, through the drive-through window, past the face of the driver, and hit the Mother in the aorta, killing her in 7 seconds. The child was unharmed. Rosemary and I reluctantly visited the site in Las Vegas because that is the place that the gang members were transacting drug deals with the employees on duty. Rosemary was the plaintiff's expert, and the case did not go to trial. It was settled.

Not Even Safe in a Hospital Bed

A 75-year-old woman, sleeping in bed on the fourth floor of an up-scale hospital in an a Las Vegas suburb, awakened to find a man on top of her, fondling her   He was pulled off her, cornered, and beaten by a very brave and angry Philippine nurse. The homeless man had been taken by ambulance to the suburban hospital because the downtown trauma centers were too overwhelmed. When they released him, he went to Room 404, instead of leaving the hospital and assaulted the elderly woman. We were defending the hospital, arguing that the suburban hospital was not prepared for the urban homeless population and would not be expected to be. The case did not go to trial and was settled.

Saved by a Bird

The female tenant, sleeping in a downtown San Diego flophouse, was attacked and beaten by another tenant. He had been released that day by the jail system. The attempted rape was averted by the entrance of her large, white, screaming cockatiel, who came from under the bed. The terrified perpetrator fled, but of course was arrested and later convicted, because she knew who he was, since he lived across the hall from her. We were defending the flop house. The civil case did not go to trial but rather settled in the early 2000s.

Murder in Broad Daylight

Then there was another horrible incident with a black woman who was clerking her mid-day shift at a kiosk gas station in Alabama in the 1990s. A black man with a gym bag entered the kiosk. He immediately locked both doors, and then proceeded to decapitate her behind the counter with a saw, a knife, and a hatchet. He rose up occasionally to tell customers through the pass-through window they were closed for the day. It was all caught on camera. The perpetrator had been released from a California mental facility and found his way to Alabama and this station on a Saturday morning. We were defending the station, and the case did not go to trial, but settled.

Fast Food Uniform

In Texas, in the 1990s, the mother of a 32-year-old-mentally-challenged young man would faithfully put on his Fast Food uniform every evening, ready for his night shift at the restaurant. He was so proud of his job. He was not trained to be a manager, but the real manager told him he had to leave for a while and he was putting the young man in charge. The manager had set it up so that, during his absence, his buddy walked in with a gun, took all of the money and then shot and killed the young man. After 13 years of service, he was buried in his Fast Food uniform, at his mother's request. The drama does indeed continue after the criminal case ends. We were defending the Fast Food restaurant, but the case did not go to trial; it settled.

Another Robbery Gone Bad

The stories go on and on from every corner of the country. Some even have a macabre humorous tone to them. Like the night in Newark, NJ when two Hispanic young men decided to rob a convenience store. Because it was a spontaneous event, neither had a disguise handy, not a gang rag or anything. So, the first one in pulled his baseball cap down low, and the second, lacking a cap, reached back and pulled his t-shirt up over his head to cover his face, exposing his entire back to the camera. Over 100 calls were registered at Crime-Stoppers the next morning, from people who recognized Josiah's shoulder to shoulder to belt-line tattoo of *Our Lady of Guadalupe*. Unfortunately, they did shoot and kill the clerk. The civil suit, in the early 2000s, in which we were defending the station, did not go to trial, but rather, it settled.

Menace II Society Copycat

In the rolling hills south of Pittsburgh and north of Washington, Pennsylvania, white painted fences section off fields of green and trees, which have shaded the hills since before the Civil War left its mark on the countryside. Homes are huge, brick and set back in the oaks at the end of sweeping drives. This is horse country, and we're not talking about the great American quarter horse. This is the home of the thoroughbred and the Tennessee Walker. You would think "No crime in this neighborhood," and you would be right. Good people live here, middle class and up. These are not homeless, no racial tension, and no poverty.

A black family, the Stevens family lived a quiet, middle-class successful life. Ev, the father, owned his own insurance company. Florence the mother, was an RN, as was their daughter Camille. The Stevens boy had the world laid out if front of him. He was a star on the high school football and basketball teams, good grades and because of his sports abilities, his grades, his size and speed, he was being considered by a number of colleges and universities as football scholarship material. They were truly an all-American family, which was especially outstanding in this overwhelmingly white community because the Stevens' were black.

Carl was normal in every way. He had good friends, no enemies, girls thought he was cool. Teachers liked his seriousness and eager participation in class and he was admired by everyone in his senior class.

In the spring, a movie was released that changed his life. He and his friends went to see Menace II Society and it had an impact on all of them. The theme announced by a well-known great actor at the beginning of the film, was to encourage young, black males to stay straight, don't do drugs, gangs, crime of any kind. Most of the kids picked up on this message. Carl did not. There was only one episode that made an impact on his mind.

At the beginning of the film, two young, black males were robbing a liquor store. As they were leaving, the wife of the owner, both Asians, said, "Your mother would not be proud of you" to which one of the perps said, "What did you say about my Mama?", and shot her and her husband to death.

Some part of Carl's sociopathic/psychopathic nature was awakened and from then on he lived with only one goal – he must kill an Asian clerk.

He bought the DVD and watched it over 40 times, according to his friends. It was the only CD that he played in his car. He carried his Dad's 12 gauge shotgun in the trunk of his car. His friends worried about him.

The Asian clerk was working the graveyard shift at a convenience store/gas station that Thursday night. It was very quiet at 0300 at the store which was located at the junction of two highways. The customers would start arriving at 0600 when they pulled in to fill up their BMW's and Lexus' on their way to work.

His neighbor and friend who suffered from insomnia and often walked over to the c-store to play chess with his friend to pass the time in the late hours of the night.

Only later, at the trial did we find out that Carl usually cruised at night looking for an Asian clerk, so it was a surprise when the bell rang and they turned to find a very tall, handsome, well-dressed young black man standing in the door holding a shotgun. Not a word was said by anyone. It was over in seconds. Carl raised the gun, shot the clerk in the face, nearly decapitating him, turned and walked back to his car. His dream had come true.

Of course the friend immediately called 911 and a police patrol stopped Carl, who surrendered peacefully. He is now serving a life sentence in, instead of playing football for a college.

Rosemary's role in the civil case in the 2000s was defending the service station in a lawsuit brought by the clerk's family. It did not go to trial. It settled.

Quadruple Homicide at a Video Store

Wednesday night was league night at the Bowling Alley in Alabama. Cars from three different states filled the parking lots. As part of the night's ritual, the Mitchell brothers, Tom 18 and Owen 17 went to a video store to get a movie while their Dad Oliver picked up a pizza.

After delivering the pizza to his house and turning on the TV, Oliver was surprised after a few minutes, when Tom and Owen did not pull in right behind him. Hearing police sirens in the distance he sat down on the front porch to wait.

At the video store, lights on the police cars gave a surreal, glow to the crime scene. Through the comments of witnesses and the CCTV, the story was told.

Todd Ryan, the manager and Les Thompson, the clerk, were beginning the closing procedure, Ryan in the back office and Thompson working the front counter. The only customers in the store were the Mitchell brothers, back in the last row, picking out a DVD.

Harvey Mann was an unemployed, alcoholic, and knew he was dying of cancer. He was very angry with the world and his circumstances. He entered the store carrying a 9mm Smith & Wesson. He shot Les without warning at the register, moved without pausing and shot Todd Ryan, coming down the steps from the office. He turned right at the back wall, and he shot the Mitchell brothers trapped in the back row.

Without saying a word, without taking cash or merchandise, Harvey Mann exited, walked back to his run-down car, where his girlfriend waited, and drove away to the hills where he lived up some crick or hollow. He knew he had cancer and indeed died in prison three months later. In the civil suit, Rosemary defended the store. The civil case did not go to trial, and was settled in the 2000s.

Rape in a Small Southern Town

Just after dark, a young black man crawled into the back seat of a 4-door car, waiting at an ATM in a small southern town outside of Jackson, Mississippi. The driver was at the machine, the passenger sitting in the car. They drove off. The CCTV caught the whole transaction.

After a time, the girls entered the City Police Department screaming that they had been raped by a black man who forced his way into their car. The girls were rushed to local hospitals for rape kits and counseling.

Meanwhile, the City Chief of Police, who was the father of one of the victims. knew just where to find the perpetrator. He was a small-time drug dealer, and off and on boyfriend, of the Chief's daughter. He claims that none of this happened. It was just a regular night--he provided them some weed and they did their thing in the backseat.

We got involved in this civil case when they filed a claim against the bank for not providing a safe environment leading to the abduction, rape, etc. The attorney working with us for defense of the bank was a quiet, competent young black female lawyer. She served as our escort for the day. As we drove out of Jackson, she pointed out the house where Medgar Evers was assassinated in 1963. Arnie said, "Man I never thought I'd get to see the driveway where Medgar Evers died" Rosemary said to the attorney: "Things have really changed since then, haven't they?" The attorney was silent for a moment, and then quietly said, "Things haven't changed a whole lot."

We waited for three hours to see our client, the bank manager, who never did show up, and we were defending him. The CCTV that had been turned over to the PD had mysteriously disappeared--for the tapes, paperwork and rape kit at the hospital. The girls dropped charges against the bank, but the rapist got a "hard 40" in prison after his sentencing, his Mama said, "This didn't make sense. Those kids were together all the time." At his trial, the alleged rapist said: "Be quiet Mama. You just sit down."

The civil case languished for a while and did not go to trial. Rosemary was defending the bank, and the case settled. She called the attorney, and he said. "Well now, that civil case is settled, and the rapist is serving his "hard 40." The black, female attorney? She's no longer with us. Not sure where she went. His Mama seems to have moved on too, or disappeared anyway. The girls are doing just fine. Oh yeah, the banker. . . Well, everything's just great down here, so, next time y'all have business down here in Jackson, we'll have another plate of that "sisters" chicken behind the court house."

Nina Simone's first song from the segregation days still works today – "Mississippi – GOD DAMN!"

TIPS FOR SAFETY

Attorney Gloria Allred and I appeared on the Dr. Phil Show together to discuss a hotel sexual assault and a bank robbery. After my appearance on the show, my tips for safety were posted on the website, as shown below.[62] I give similar advice at seminars, particularly for women traveling alone, but men are at risk in hotels also.

Tips for Hotel Safety

Dr. Phil's guest, New York businesswoman Alison, is suing a hotel in Finland on allegations that she was sexually assaulted when the front desk gave her room key to a man claiming to be her husband. Dr. Rosemary Erickson is a security expert who teaches seminars on hotel safety for businesswomen. Here are her tips for staying safe while in hotels:

- Tell front desk your main concern is security.
- Never get a room on the ground floor.
- Try to avoid rooms where balconies connect.
- Don't get an adjoining room.
- Never prop your door open to go to the ice machine.
- Always use the deadbolt and make sure windows are locked.
- Make sure you know the person knocking on your door. If they say they work for the hotel, get their name and call the front desk and double check. Make sure there is a reason why they're sending an electrician/housekeeper, etc., to your room.
- Have a doorman escort you to your room at night.
- Be mindful of long hallways or corners you can't see around.
- If you see someone you're unsure of on the floor of your room, turn around and get back on the elevator — try again later. There's something known as "push and shove:" when you insert your electronic key, an assailant then shoves you into the room and closes the door. It's the easiest way for a rapist to get into your room.

What to Do During a Bank Robbery

Dr. Phil's guest, Rich, found himself in a bank during an attempted armed robbery in 2010. When the bank robber made a move to jump over the counter, Rich tackled him and held the man until police arrived. Even though he got shot in the leg in the process, Rich was very lucky.

Dr. Rosemary Erickson is a security expert who trains bank employees in what to do during a robbery. Here are her Dos and Don'ts if you find yourself at a bank during an attempted robbery:

Do:

- Cooperate
- Give up the money
- Obey the robber's commands
- Keep your hands in sight

Don't:

- Resist
- Talk
- Plead
- Stare
- Make any sudden movements
- Be a hero
- Chase or follow

Dr. Erickson says most bank robberies are over in 90 seconds and only 4 percent of robberies end up with injured victims. Of those, 82 percent are due to someone resisting. Bottom line: Don't be a hero. [End Dr. Phil website].

When being vigilant fails, or security measures do not prevent a violent crime, then law enforcement takes over. The Epilogue is my tribute to law enforcement and the important role they play in these violent crime cases.

EPILOGUE

This Epilogue is largely about the death of a deputy in my home county, where I grew up in South Dakota. It is my personal tribute to law enforcement for not only their involvement with my research through my entire career, but their excellent work in investigating and writing up criminal cases, which help in the civil cases, as well as for the risks they take every day. Many of my compatriots in the security business and loss prevention field were former law enforcement, and I greatly respect their service to society. The death of a deputy sheriff in my hometown county was one of those dedicated public servants.

The deaths of those we know and love, and sometimes even the death of strangers, can make a difference to us. There are also deaths in our lives that are not just about the loss of the individuals but about how the events change everything—in recent times, we think of John F. Kennedy and Martin Luther King, and of the thousands killed on 9/11 in 2001, and the shooting of over 500 people in Las Vegas in 2017, who were attending a country music concert. We remember where we were on those days, and those deaths shook us to the core. With those deaths, we lost our sense of security and safety and life as we knew it.

Historically, such an event was the assassination of Julius Caesar. On March 15th, 44 B.C, Julius Caesar was assassinated on what is known as the "Ides of March." Since that time that day has always held a sense of foreboding, and the assassination itself changed Rome forever. Shakespeare's *Julius Caesar* was not written until a century and half later in 1599, but in its creation the event was kept alive for centuries to come. In the play, we are reminded that a soothsayer had warned Caesar of the potential danger with the now famous line of: "Beware the Ides of March." On that day, Portia had asked the time, and the soothsayer replies "About the ninth hour, lady." She asks if Caesar has gone to the Capitol, and he replies that he has not. Then, when Caesar sees the soothsayer, he says: "The ides of March are come". And the soothsayer replies," "Ay, Caesar, but not gone."

Shortly thereafter, the conspirators and other senators take their places and stab Caesar, Casca first, Brutus last, and Caesar says: "Et tu, Brute?" and dies. Afterwards, Brutus says "That we shall die, we know; 'tis but the time and drawing days out that men stand upon." Caesar had earlier said that "Cowards die many times before their deaths: The valiant never taste of death but once."

In 2009, I would experience a death that would have a great impact on me, and it happened at the very same day and hour. Little did I know that our young deputy in Turner County, where I grew up, should have had the same warning that the soothsayer had given to Caesar—"Beware the Ides of March." For on the morning, of March 15th, 2009, at the ninth hour, Turner County Deputy Chad Mechels was murdered in the line of duty. It is no exaggeration to say that his death would change Turner County forever because with the murder of the deputy, we lost our innocence, and the sense of security that we had always enjoyed. A law enforcement officer had never been murdered in Turner County, and it had been over twenty years since a law enforcement officer had been murdered in the state of South Dakota.

The night before, my brother Dean, a Deputy Sheriff in Turner County, was at our cabin on Swan Lake (also right in Turner County). We gave him an article about the first known gang recorded right in our county, located just a few miles from Centerville, South Dakota. Earlier that week, it was also reported that Mexican drug cartels had found their way to Sioux Falls, South Dakota. Both of these events were new, out of character, and disturbing for our area.

The next morning, on March 15th, 2009, at 8:45am, I was opening the drapes of our home on the lake, where Arnie and I were staying for the weekend. I sat there, drinking my cup of French Press Pot Italian Roast coffee, while listening to the geese fly north overhead--always an encouraging sign of spring in Turner County. I would not know until hours later what events would transpire within minutes, just fifteen miles away to the north and east of our cabin. At 8:52am, a 911 call went into the dispatcher for Turner County, who was located in Canton, SD, saying that someone had a gun and was threatening suicide.

The dispatcher sent out the only Turner County deputy that was on duty on a Sunday morning—Deputy Chad Mechels. At 9:10 A.M, Deputy Chad Mechels reported to the dispatcher "I'm here." At 9:15 am, a 911 call went into a different area with a different dispatcher in Mitchell saying "I'm Ethan Johns, and a deputy has been shot." Responding to that call was the Turner County Sheriff. He arrived at 9:47am, and found Deputy Mechels on the ground outside his Turner County Sheriff's SUV. Byron radioed for help, and Deputy Mechels was airlifted to Avera McKennan Hospital in Sioux Falls where he died that afternoon.

According to the first court documents released, when Deputy Mechels responded to the call, Ethan Johns, it turns out, was armed with a rifle and repeatedly opened fire on Turner County Deputy Chad Mechels when he arrived. Johns, who was 19, was in the bathroom at his farmhouse when he first shot Mechels, wounding the lawman in the right arm. After the deputy retreated from the house and climbed back into his patrol SUV, Johns opened fire again from the bathroom window with a high-powered deer rifle and shot him through the windshield in the throat--a fatal wound.

The night preceding the slaying, Johns had altercations with his girlfriend first in Sioux Falls and later at his girlfriend's home in Parker--the county seat. The parents of the girlfriend called police when Johns refused to leave their residence. As a result, law enforcement began actively searching for Johns. Meanwhile, according to an affidavit in the initial case, against Johns, he exchanged text messages with his girlfriend's sister. She told him that police were coming to talk to him. At 2:51pm that Sunday morning, Johns sent a return text message to her saying "That's fucking up to u if they come over I'm shooting them and me hope that I feel better." How much of that background did Deputy Mechels have when he went out on the call? Did it go to him as a welfare check, as first reported? Did it go to him as a suicide threat? Did he know the subject was armed? Did he know Johns had threatened to kill law enforcement if they came over to his place?

Johns had been in trouble with the Turner County law enforcement and the criminal justice system since he was fourteen. His parents lived in Parker, and he graduated from Parker High School. At this point, however, he lived alone a few miles away from Parker, on a dairy farm near Marion, South Dakota. He worked as a hired hand, and in exchange for his work, as part of his remuneration, he lived in the house on one of his employer's two farms. His employer described him as a "good boy." I find the criminals usually are described that way, especially by their mothers, and the employer had no idea that Johns would ever be violent. He reports that Johns was interested in joining the military. I wish he had.

I was so stricken after this happened, that for the next week, I would wake up at night crying and thinking "Our poor little deputy is dead." I could only think of him as "Our poor little deputy," though in fact he was a 32-year-old married man with two children, ages 7 and 3. Deputy Mechels was born and raised in Turner County. It was reportedly his life-long dream to be a Deputy Sheriff in Turner County, and he had been in the job only 5 1/2 months, since October 2008. The pain I felt was also for my brother, Dean, who had been a deputy there for 30 years, and was on the crime scene the entire day. At 71 years of age, he must have thought "It could have been me," and with his altruistic nature, he probably went so far as to think he wished it could have been him, rather than a young man with his entire life ahead of him.

Dean, one autumn day a few years before, sat for three hours in a pick-up truck in a field with a farmer, who held a shotgun in his lap the entire time, threatening suicide. When those calls came in, and when the dispatch was handled locally in Parker, Dean was the one that would usually be called to "talk them down." But that didn't happen on the Ides of March in 2009. Only the week before, Deputy Mechels had provided training to his fellow officers on responding to similar situations—how you should always have something between you and the shooter—a bathroom door wasn't enough, when he was in the house, however, and neither was the windshield of the SUV enough when he tried to leave.

These are the kinds of questions everyone asked at the debriefing after the murder. All of the deputies, and everyone involved, from dispatch on, wondered what they might have done differently. How could you not wonder? Would the outcome have been different if my brother Dean would have taken the call, or would my Dean be the one we would be mourning? Instead it was Deputy Chad Mechels that was to be deeply mourned by his fellow officers. In services held at the Dakota Prairie Playhouse in Madison, South Dakota, hundreds of fellow officers from every corner of South Dakota came along with officers from Nebraska and the Minnesota. Hundreds of patrol cars lined the road for two miles leading to the cemetery, where Deputy Mechels was buried on a warm and sunny day for South Dakota on March 18, 2009.

From the Ohio Buckeye's Sheriff's Association, a poem is posted for fellow officers killed in the line of duty called "A Part of America Died." With the death of Turner County Deputy Sheriff Chad Mechels, a part of Turner County died.

"A Part of America Died"

Somebody killed a Policeman today,
and a part of America died.
A piece of our country he swore to protect,
will be buried with him at his side.

The suspect that shot him will stand up in court,
with counsel demanding his rights.
While a young widowed mother must work for her kids,
and spend many long, lonely nights.

The beat that he walked was a battle field too,
just as if he'd gone off to war.
Though the flag of our nation won't fly at half mast,
to his name they will add a gold star.

Yes, somebody killed a policeman today,
in your hometown or in mine.
While we slept in comfort behind our locked doors,

Now his ghost walks a beat on a dark city street,
and he stands at each rookies side.

EPILOGUE

He answered the call, of himself gave his all,
And A Part Of America Died.

At the funeral, a poem included these words: "I hope I did my job well. I pray I was fighting when I fell." He did his job well, and he was fighting when he fell. Newspapers from coast to coast from Palm Beach to San Francisco to Seattle covered the story of the shooting death of a Deputy Sheriff from rural South Dakota. It was covered in the *Las Vegas Sun, New York Times, Seattle Times, Seattle P-I, Miami Post*, the Associated Press, internet sites, and myriad blogs. The Governor of South Dakota ordered that flags across the state be flown at half-staff on the day of the deputy's funeral. The Governor attended the funeral and reminded people of the willingness of law enforcement officers to place themselves in danger to protect society every day when they go to work. That is what everyone in the state was feeling.

Traffic was backed up for eight miles on Highway 34 fully two hours before the funeral was to begin, and traffic is virtually never backed up anywhere in South Dakota. This fact alone, showed the impact of this rare event of the slaying of a law enforcement officer in the rural Midwest. A local limousine service donated their limousines for the family members to make their way from the funeral to the cemetery. The Sheriff of Turner County said that for him it was like losing a child to lose one of his men. Deputy Mechels was remembered as a loving son, father, and husband, and his co-workers thought he was "a great kid." Thousands of people sent messages of sympathy to the various web sites set up to receive them, and generous donations were made through the Wells Fargo Bank, who set up a special Chad Mechels Memorial fund for Chad's wife and two children.

At the funeral, *Jesus Loves Me* was played, especially for his children, and reporters say there was not a dry eye in the place, including those of the law enforcement who sat quietly, stoically, in their seats at the funeral. Later they would salute the casket as it made its way slowly to the cemetery, and the patrol cars and motorcycles would line the country road for two miles. The month of March in South Dakota is always bleak. There are no leaves on the trees, no green in the fields or in the grass, and there are miles and miles of unrelenting flat gray-brown prairie. The prairie can be a lonely place for the living, but even lonelier in death.

Why, instead of just one deputy responding to the call, couldn't it have been like another call received a few years earlier? Dean invited two other deputies for breakfast at his farm. The farm is just a mile south of Hwy 18 going into Davis, South Dakota. They got together at about 2am, after duty, on a Sunday morning. The deputies all had their police radios on the table and were listening to calls, while eating their sausage, pancakes, and eggs. They kept eating because none of the incidents on the police radio being reported were in Turner County...not yet anyway. The police radio information was this: Twelve miles to the east on Interstate Highway 29, a South Dakota Highway Patrolman had attempted to stop someone who was speeding. A high-speed chase ensued, with what we would later learn was a drug runner, who was running drugs from Omaha, Nebraska to Sioux Falls, South Dakota. Not knowing where he was, the drug runner, in a fairly new white Cadillac, turned west on Highway 18, which meant he was headed straight for Davis, right past where the Turner County Deputies were eating breakfast on Dean's farm. With the word that he was coming their way, they all simultaneously pushed back their chairs, re-arranged their guns in their holsters, put their radios back on their belts, and headed for their SUVs.

In the meantime, the drug runner, who was from out of state, originally out of the country, and therefore completely unfamiliar with South Dakota, must have thought turning west on Highway 18 and off of the Interstate would be a good idea for getting away. What he did not know, is that by the time he went 10 miles west, there would be three Turner County Sheriff SUVs lined up with lights flashing, as he whizzed past them at the stop sign, going 70 mph. The deputies joined in the high speed pursuit, through Davis (population 100). Just past Davis, the drug runner took a sharp, fast turn to the right on what he assumedly thought was a road, but it was only a driveway that would dead-end in a field.

Once he hit the dead end, he jumped out of his Cadillac and

took off on foot, running through the field toward the river bed. All three deputies and the additional highway patrol officers, who had picked up the chase, took out on foot through the field after him. In the lead was the oldest one of all at 60+ years of age. That would be former Centerville high school track runner, Dean Erickson. Dean, with his flashlight, was able to find the 28-year-old suspect hiding under the brush and tackled him into the riverbed. Dean's words to him were: "Your first mistake was speeding; your second mistake was coming to Turner County." I later asked Dean what the drug runner's race or nationality was, and he said "Well, he wasn't Norwegian". Diversity was coming to South Dakota.

I have been fortunate to have the upbringing, educational advantages, travel, and good luck to be involved in researching up close and personal some of the most interesting and worst criminal violence this country has known. I wish I could say things have been getting better, but they haven't. After the peak in crime in 1991, most statisticians, criminologists, government agencies, law enforcement, and the media compare whatever has happened since then as "a decline in crime since 1991". That is not *incorrect*, but it is the nature, seriousness, and type of violent crime that has changed. In the early 2000s, I had predicted there would be more mass shootings and multiple victim shootings, and that is what, unfortunately, has happened, in recent years. I will, however, always hope for a safer future for our society, as did Cicero, over two thousand years ago, when he said:

The safety of the people shall be the highest law.

About the Author

Rosemary J. Erickson, Ph.D. grew up on a farm in South Dakota and went on to become a nationally renowned expert witness on violent crime. She received a B.A. in psychology at Augustana University in Sioux Falls, South Dakota. She later received her M.A. in Sociology at San Diego State University, and then her Ph.D. in Sociology: Justice at the American University in Washington, D. C. She has taught at the American University and San Diego State University. She has also consulted and trained corporations and government agencies worldwide in crime prevention and written other books on crime and its causes. *Prairie Patriarch: A Farmer's Daughter Becomes an Expert Witness on Violent Crime* was written by Dr. Erickson some years ago. It was only recently published to provide the backdrop for this book. *Prairie Patriarch* is about Dr. Erickson's "roots" and the part her father, mother, and rural upbringing brought about in developing her character, values, determination, and interest in researching and testifying about violent crime. Because this book is written by a sociologist, it is believed to be suitable as a supplementary text for the sociology, criminology, law enforcement, or law student interested in crime and the criminal justice system, and a behind-the-scenes look at the life of a female expert witness on violent crime.

Other Books by Rosemary J. Erickson, Ph.D.

- *Paroled but Not Free,* Human Sciences Press, Behavioral Publications: NY. 1973.
- *Armed Robbers and Their Crimes,* Athena Research Corporation: Seattle, WA. 1996..
- *The Use of Social Science Data in Supreme Court Decisions,* University of Illinois Press: Chicago. 1998.
- *Prairie Patriarch: A Farmers Daughter Becomes an Expert Witness on Violent Crime.* Amazon.com/createspace.com, 2017.
- Related Chapter in a Book: "Target Selection by Criminal Groups and Gang's" in *Handbook of Forensic Sociology and Psychology* by Stephen J. Morewitz and Mark L. Goldstein. Springer Publication: NY, 2014.

Athena's website, which includes Dr. Erickson's vita, is at www.AthenaResearch.com.
Dr. Erickson's author website can be found at www.RosemaryJErickson.com

Notes

[1] *Return to Laughter.* Elenore Smith Bowen. Random House, NY: 1954 & Doubleday: 1964.

[2] *Beat the Dealer.* Edward O. Thorp. Vintage Books: 1966.

[3] Crow, Wayman J. & Bull, James L. 1975. *Robbery Deterrence: An Applied Behavioral Science Demonstration.* Western Behavioral Sciences Institute. La Jolla, CA.

[4] Crow, Wayman J., Erickson, Rosemary J. and Scott, Lloyd. September, 1987. "Set Your Sights". *Security Management.* Vol. 31, No. 9 & data provided by The Southland Corporation.

[5] The robbery prison study was supported by Athena Research Corporation and 7-Eleven, Inc. Further details and findings from the studies with full references can be found on line under *Teenage Robbers* at www.athenaresearch.com.

[6] *Teenage Robbers* is available online at www.athenaresearch.com.

[7] Erickson, Rosemary J. and Simon, Rita J. *The Use of Social Science Data in Supreme Court Decisions.* University of Illinois Press: Urbana, IL: 1998

[8] Erickson, R. J. *Social Science and the Law.* American University Dissertation, 1994. P. 15. References are listed in the dissertation for the concepts within the table but the individuals have no responsibility for the juxtaposition or characterizations.

[9] Jenna Brownson. *Huffpost.* 5/26/2016. Rodney King's actual quote was "Can we all get along?" It has been quoted differently over time.

[10] From Thomas Sowell's *A Conflict of Visions* (1987)

[11] Pinker, Steven. *The Blank Slate.* Viking: 2002. With additional credit to Edmund Burke for the tragic vision and Jean-Jacques Rosseau for the utopian vision.

[12] R. J. & Crow, W. J. "Violence in business settings". *The American Behavioral Scientist* 23(5), 717-742.

[13] "Target Selection by Criminal Groups and Gangs". S. J. Morewitz and M.L. Goldstein (eds.) *Handbook of Forensic Sociology and Psychology.* Springer:NY. 2014.

[14] For a discussion of CPTED, see Hunter, Ronald D. and Jeffery, C. Ray. *Preventing Convenience Store Robbery through Environmental Design.* 1992.

[15] The research on these measures can be found by Erickson in *Convenience Store Security at the Millennium* available from www.nacsonline.com.

[16] Erickson, R. J. *Teenage Robbers.* www.athenaresearch.com.

[17] Erickson, R. J. *Teenage Robbers.* www.athenaresearch.com.

[18] The research on these measures can be found by Erickson in *Convenience Store Security at the Millennium* available from www.nacsonline.com.

[19] https://www.osha.gov/Publications/osha3153.pdf.

[20]https://www.google.com/url?sa=t&rct=j&q=&esrc=s&source=web&cd=1&cad=rja&uact=8&ved=0ahUKEwi41PrYpZvWAhViwVQKHf_4AEUQFggmMAA&url=https%3A%2F%2Fcapindex.com%2F&usg=AFQjCNHwvWkZL83qigij6WyGaZerfiaODA

[21] John Douglas. *Mass Murderers.* Website, 2007.

[22] Hare Psychopathy Checklist-Revised: 2nd Edition™

[23] Erickson, Rosemary J. and Simon, Rita J. *The Use of Social Science Data in Supreme Court Decisions.* University of Illinois Press: Urbana and Chicago. 1998.

[24] http://legal-dictionary.thefreedictionary.com/Daubert+standard

[25] https://www.forensisgroup.com/daubert-standard-for-expert-testimony

[26] Stephen Hawking, February 23, 2015 by Tanya Lewis www.livescience.com

[27] Criminal Trial State of New Mexico, Plaintiff–Appellee, v. Paul LOVETT, Defendant–Appellant. No Supreme Court of New Mexico. 30,470. Decided: August 24, 2012. [Related sections are included].

[28] Ibid.

[29] Ibid.

[30] National Drug Intelligence Center. *New Mexico Drug Threat Assessment.* April 2002

[31] There were other legislative and policy issues at stake about appropriate security measures, which are discussed in detail in other publications, such as NIOSH, OSHA, and on my website at www.athenaresearch.com.

[32] Adams, Terry, Mary Brooks-Mueller, and Scott Shaw. *Eye of the Beast*. Addicus Books: 1998. Pp. 8-17.

[33] Adams, Terry, Mary Brooks-Mueller, and Scott Shaw. *Eye of the Beast*. Addicus Books: 1998.

[34] 967 P.2d 702 (1998). 132 Idaho 88. STATE of Idaho, Plaintiff-Respondent v James E. WOOD, Defendant-Appellant. Nos. 21057, 22375. Supreme Court of Idaho, Boise, December 1996 Term. October 9, 1998. https://scholar.google.com/scholar_case?case=13054074072842052589&q=State +of+Idaho+vs.+James+Wood&hl=en&as_sdt=6,42

[35] https://www.eastidahonews.com/2016/10/pocatello-girl-remembered-23-years-after-one-of-idahos-most-horrific-crimes/https://www.eastidahonews.com/2016/10/pocatello-girl-remembered-23-years-after-one-of-idahos-most-horrific-crimes/

[36] https://www.eastidahonews.com/2016/10/pocatello-girl-remembered-23-years-after-one-of-idahos-most-horrific-crimes/

[37] https://www.eastidahonews.com/2016/10/pocatello-girl-remembered-23-years-after-one-of-idahos-most-horrific-crimes/

[38] http://maamodt.asp.radford.edu/Psyc%20405/serial%20killers/Wood,%20Jame %20Edward%20_spring%202007_.pdf

[39] Weber, Wells, and Wesley reference the following for their analysis: Adams, T., Brooks-Mueller, M., & Shaw, S. (1998). *Eye of the beast: The true story of serial killer James Wood*. Omaha, NE: Addicus Books, Inc.

[40] www.kcci.com//print/738814/detail.html. *Piper is Accused of Killing Patricia Lange*. KCCI. Channel 8. 2007.

[41] http://www.thedarksideofamerica.com/piper-donald.html.

[42] Source: FindLaw Source: Des Moines Register

[43] Source: FindLaw Source: Des Moines Register Source: FindLaw Source: Des Moines Register

[44] http://www.kcci.com/news/805978/detail.html#ixzz1nQtGSsEN

[45] http://www.kcci.com/news/805978/detail.html#ixzz1nQtMQ7oI

[46] https://iowacoldcases.org/case-summaries/mariana-redrovan/

[47] *Cedar Rapids Gazette*, Jan. 24, 1998

[48] https://cases.justia.com/iowa/court-of-appeals/02-1124-(2003-10-15).doc

[49] https://iowacoldcases.org/case-summaries/mariana-redrovan/

[50] http://www.qconline.com/news/iowa/man-arrested-in--year-old-hotel-slaying/article_ecd01c7f-4b0a-53df-a993-032170cfa3d9.html

[51] https://iowacoldcases.org/case-summaries/mariana-redrovan/

[52] http://www.qconline.com/news/iowa/man-arrested-in--year-old-hotel-slaying/article_ecd01c7f-4b0a-53df-a993-032170cfa3d9.html

[53] http://www.iasd.uscourts.gov/sites/default/files/opinions/401cv40498_0502.pdf

[54] Ibid. p. 8.

[55] www.fbi.gov

[56] www.fbi.gov

[57] Hare, Robert. D. "Antisocial Personality, Sociopathy, and Psychopathy". www.faculty.ncwc.edu. P. 7.

[58] http://twistedminds.creativescapism.com/serial-killers-introduction/

[59] http://www.nampn.org/cases/burns_samantha.html

[60] Hare, Robert D. "Antisocial Personality, Sociopathy, and Psychopathy". www.faculty.ncwc.edu. P. 7.

[61] www.psychological.com

[62] *CBS Dr. Phil.* "Behind the Headlines". May 28, 2012.

Made in the USA
Las Vegas, NV
28 July 2023

75337067R00140